WHO WANTS IT?

WHO WANTS IT?

COLIN WARD AND
'CHUBBY' CHRIS HENDERSON

MAINSTREAM
PUBLISHING

EDINBURGH AND LONDON

First published in Great Britain in 2000 by
MAINSTREAM PUBLISHING COMPANY (EDINBURGH) LTD
7 Albany Street
Edinburgh EH1 3UG

ISBN 1 84018 325 X

This edition, 2002
Reprinted 2003

A catalogue record for this book is available from the British Library

Typeset in Block and Janson Text
Printed and bound in Great Britain by Mackays of Chatham plc

Forget what you've read in the papers or seen on the TV – and that's plenty.
This is the true, uncut story of what being a Chelsea Headhunter was really about, as told to Colin Ward by Chris Henderson.

CONTENTS

INTRODUCTION

ONE GROUP OF FOOTBALL FANS, the Chelsea Headhunters, has assumed mythical status to other fans. To this day, the mere mention of their name strikes fear into many citizens. Chris Henderson formed the Chelsea Headhunters as well as the band Combat 84, the antithesis of middle-class England with its raw, uncut punk lyrics and affiliation to the philosophy of George Orwell. While the band never achieved lasting fame, the same cannot be said of the Chelsea Headhunters, who earned a reputation as the most dangerous thugs in Britain and were seen, along with the ICF, as the most feared in Europe, with governments taking an interest in them. After Stephen 'Hickey' Hickmott's shock jailing in 1986, Chris took on the mantle of organising a small group of Chelsea fans who travelled to matches by luxury coach. This style epitomised the travelling domestic fan who also tended to travel extensively abroad with England in the mid-1980s. No more British Rail Specials or budget coach journeys – this was the era of designer dressing and designed violence. Old meeting places were reinstated and flare gun and gas attacks were played out to a backdrop of the new post-punk music scene.

Chris and his gang were part of the second wave of high profile mass arrests, and their show trial was engineered to be the crowning glory of Thatcher's corrupt and systematic squashing of football hooligans once and for all. But it was the dramatic collapse of this trial that sounded the death knell for the undercover police operations and indiscriminate arrests and jailings.

Violence surrounded the Chelsea fans long before Chris Henderson came on the scene, but the media interest in the sinister reputation of the Headhunters made all those associated with the game public enemy number one. This is the captivating story of the era of music and football, when the way you looked counted as much as how you performed.

REVELLING IN IT

THE HUGE SCRAPBOOK WAS LAID OUT across the living-room table. The colour of the newspaper cuttings with their curled-up edges had long since faded and yellowed. The words shame, scum, disgrace and, with time, animals headed every article, almost as if those written about were not real people at all, but actors performing a role. As each page was turned, the musty smell of old newspaper stored too long in a winter loft wafted around the room. The jubilant defiance of youth shone out from every page. The cuttings depicted other times and places, many different fashions, but the actors had the same faces, only now they were older. Age hadn't diminished their influence or their place in history; nothing could do that.

Even now, as the pages were slowly turned, those reading the clippings laughed at the antics described and felt the same buzz as dramatic headlines were relived – mass anarchy, the end of a football match transformed into a pitch invasion, a fight, a kick in the head; preferably his, not yours. Nothing had changed. The headlines still shocked after 20 years. Youth culture was ever thus: measuring yourself against somebody else. In the case of hooligans, the tradition of going up against other firms would never change, even if the faces did.

Now the boys had received a wake-up call of monumental

proportions. There wasn't one of them who didn't breathe in sharply when they heard the sentences. Life, ten years. Along with the pain came a condemnation from the Ministry (the media and conformist society in general) and a pat on the back for those who had dished it out. This wasn't some petty skirmish outside the Fulham Broadway tube where a few guys ran and left the others to take a kicking. No – this was a lights-out Iron Curtain call of 1945 proportions. 'You're not telling us we're telling you, we are the mob and we'll chase you until there's no breath left in your body, then as you collapse on the floor we'll give you the full Monty attack.' Not just the main faces, but every last one who'd dared to even be there observing. In the end, the guys who were going down were real bodies, first-class mates – not arseholes from somewhere else who deserved it – we knew and drank with them.

Every one of us could recount at least one tale of our exploits together. For years, there had been nothing but the firm and our mates and the belief that people who stand together are looked up to. We were lads, free to wander and enjoy ourselves in station concourses, mean, uncompromising, dirty streets and favoured drinking haunts, nodding acknowledgements to our mates.

The Ministry had spent years telling us our days were numbered, that something had to be done, but who could do anything? Weren't we unstoppable? While they preached our demise, we laughed at their temerity to suggest that we were living on borrowed time. Now they were shutting the prison doors on the lads faster than we could run.

The graffiti ghosts of the 1970s who had proclaimed George Davis innocent of armed robbery from every bridge in London were needed again, yet everywhere the faces shook their heads, threw up their hands and cried *en masse*: go on you shitters, become spectres entering a twilight world of fear and loathing. Eventually a familiar face might emerge from the shadows, as if those who were imprisoned were calling upon you to make a stand.

We couldn't hide – the siren call of combat was too strong for us, beckoning us forward. We weren't tied to the mast as Ulysses was. All we could do was ask ourselves who 'they' were, whether they would be waiting and what they had in store for us. If there was no hiding place. For years now, the Ministry had barked out their propaganda; that the politicians had all the answers while we shouted that Queen Victoria was alive and manning a market stall down Petticoat Lane – silly quotes from sillier old bastards. Well, now we'd better start believing them.

Paul Scarrott was a nutter in every sense of the word, undoubtedly two beers short of a six pack. He was completely barking long before the Ministry dubbed him England's public enemy number one. Scarrott was old school, and had been around long enough to still sing the Middle of the Road-derivative song: 'Oh Tweedle Dee, Oh Tweedle Dum; We are the Forest and we never run'. With his little moustache adding definition to a lived-in face and NFFC (Nottingham Forest Football Club) tattoos, including the word FOREST tattooed inside his bottom lip, he looked rough, yet despite his strong physique he was harmless in everyday life and completely useless in a row, although he worked as a bouncer in and around Nottingham and was a legend.

Scarrott never ran, usually because he was too pissed. His sole aim in life seemed to be to lay waste to Europe's drink stock and get himself arrested or punched out by our continental cousins. His reasoning was simple: 'We hate anyone who isn't British. They're scum and we let them know it.' Scarrott, like many other fans, used the word 'we' to describe his culture. While Scarrott wasn't the main protagonist, he became one of the most visible exponents of the soccer violence culture for many years – the *bête noir* of the *Daily Mail* and anti-Christ of the reasoning middle classes. In 1981, Scarrott tagged along with a group of Chelsea fans travelling to Switzerland. No sooner had he got off the ferry at Ostend than he walked across the road, picked up the nearest bicycle he could find and threw it through a shop window. 'You're all fuckin' collaborators,' he shouted. 'Pseudo-Germans, sit on your arses waiting for the English to liberate you.' Then, calm as you like, he strolled back across the road as if nothing had happened.

Everybody wanted a pound for the amount of times Scarrott had felt the lash of a police truncheon, for the call of Europe, be it Nottingham Forest or England, was too much for him to resist. Even when he stayed at home, controversy and bad luck dogged him. During the 1986 Mexico World Cup, he had ordered a Chinese takeaway while watching the early group matches. When England conceded a goal, he threw his plate of food straight out of the window and happened to hit a passing pedestrian. Arrest and infamy – the only football hooligan arrested for a solo assault from his front room. 'LOCAL SOCCER THUG KNOCKS OUT OLD LADY' was how the press described it.

'I can't handle it any more,' he once said when he came back from yet another police beating, this time in Belgium while watching his beloved Nottingham Forest play Anderlecht, where he'd thrown the beer bottle he was drinking from at an Anderlecht player and hit him. The locals shouted their displeasure, then ran over and gave him a kicking, while the local police watched until he'd received a decent punishment then dragged him out, arrested him and for good measure gave him a welting across his back. They produced him in court the next morning complete with dried bloodstains on his shirt. He received a six-month sentence.

'Poxy Belgian wankers, no bloody gratitude to us English. It was their fault for selling me beer inside the ground.'

Every time he was released the tabloids hounded him and he never failed them. 'Wankers. Ungrateful foreigners. Thick Froggies, that's what those Belgian tossers are. Now get out of my way, I'm off to soak my bruises in beer from the inside.'

'Why did you do it, Mr Scarrott?'

'Went to Europe for a good time, had a sing-song while I got pissed with my mates and fellow fans, threw up then supported my team and somehow got into a scuffle. English people are born with natural courage. We have to charge, it's in our nature,' he would argue at the reporters who would nod in agreement, creaming their pants because they'd got their soundbite and a picture of a grinning unrepentant Scarrott, then walk away to slaughter him in print, even though his logic was so compellingly true that everybody who read it secretly nodded before tut-tutting and condemning Mr Scarrott.

Any reporter who wanted more or tried to look beneath the veneer of drink and a good time was always disappointed because that was it. The whole story could be told in two lines and was so bloody resonant that it didn't need any more added. A psychology thesis: Scarrott, PhD in drunken hooliganism. In another age, perhaps a few centuries ago, he would have been revered as a hero, fit to sit alongside Sir Lancelot. Now his reward was repugnance, making him so reviled that he received a banning order from every Watney Coombe Reid public house in Britain. Drink and football, what a combination. As Scarrott summed it up: 'I've never met anybody who refused to serve me when I'm sober, they only refuse you when you've spent 50 quid and filled your boots. They sell you wobbly juice all day then wonder why we go bonkers.' As a thesis for a master's degree it may have lacked depth, but for lads like Scarrott it made perfect sense. While we nodded in agreement the rest of England shook their heads, pretending that the beasts within them were tamed and under control.

Back in Nottingham, Scarrott was a well-known character and his local landlady in The Fountain public house, Pauline Clay, was quoted as saying that she loved him because he was charming and polite. His girlfriend was well spoken and he had a small coterie of good mates. The expression 'football fever' aptly summed up Scarrott, like anyone else who ever invaded foreign soil in support of their country. Add beer to Scarrott, light the blue touchpaper, then stand back.

By the time he had his finest hour in 1988 at the European Championships, getting deported from Germany and as a result being tagged the looniest hooligan in Britain, he had been jailed on 13 separate occasions for football-related violence, including the infamous battle of Hampden Park where he was charged with inciting a crowd to violence.

'What are you supposed to do when 1,000 William Wallaces high on the malt stuff come charging at you – hum "Flower of Scotland" and hope they calm down? Get fuckin' real.'

For good measure, he had a Stanley knife in his pocket.

'Why did you have that blade on you, Mr Scarrott?' asked the magistrate.

'I use it for cutting cables at work, your honour.'

'Six months, with three suspended. Send him down.'

───────

Funny moments, sad moments, surreal moments, which could never translate to the page or the television screen, try as you might. Mates stuck together in a time machine, never growing old. Peter Pan, every one. What do hooligans do in the close season? Like the enigma melted away, the tide receding. Who knew? Nobody cared because once we were off the front page, everybody thought we'd gone away for the last time. Then August came around once again and we regrouped and charged.

As I write, it is already a long time ago, but still the feelings are there: you need only sit in a bar with your mates and back they flood, intangible to everybody else. Seeking them out now is a farce for those who still try to chase the rainbow's end of the thrill, because what we had has gone forever. Some say it's still around, it never went, but there was never any twilight. One day it was there and the next the fun was gone.

Everywhere we went we were looking for action, something different from what we'd done before, and everywhere it happened. It never disappointed us – what we craved never failed to materialise.

On the grey London brick of the railway near Stamford Bridge at the Kings Road end, sprayed black letters loom straight from the can with the paint dripping away at the edges, not like the graffiti art you see nowadays in the inner cities. 'Elvis is Dead' someone had sprayed, then underneath, in blue and a little neater, 'Yeah, but Eccles is still King of the Shed'. How do you think that made Eccles and the rest of us feel every time we saw it? In the days when graffiti wasn't fashionable, this was a fashion statement which sat alongside the Mary Quant pictures that adorned the King's Road hoardings. Elvis may have been the king of rock and roll, but down here he was only a prince.

To drop into the conversation that you knew Eccles made you special; to say, 'Shit mate, I know Eccles', gave you real hero worship. 'You were with him down at Parsons Green the other night? Wow!' Eccles marshalling the boys, sending them one way then another, hunting down luckless rival fans. There were four Leeds boys with their scarves stuffed down the front of their trousers, pretending they were locals. As if you couldn't recognise the Chelsea football face. Eccles sorted them and took their scarves for good measure, throwing them in a dustbin further down the road. People called him the General and followed him, hung on his every word, even trailed him to the toilet to take a piss next to him. Then your mates would look at you with respect because you saw him in the street and he addressed you by name and you called him back by his real name, Harkins: that was really something. It made you somebody. 'You're two bob,' we all shouted at the opposing fans, doing the head shine sign in thousands to signify what we thought of them. Everybody else was a wanker, except for those in our group. Another time, another language: almost incomprehensible, beyond belief really.

———

'Congratulations, You've Just Met the Inter-City Firm.' Those West Ham boys made the calling card their greatest fashion accessory. They were in the pain and humiliation business, so why not carry a business card? The macabre existence of the cards was confirmed when one was found next to the dying body of an Arsenal fan after a fatal stabbing incident outside Highbury in the early 1980s. But it wasn't macabre to us: we understood where they were coming from. Calling cards and Fancy Dan names for fans linked together by the love of their team.

But what to do about a name? Everybody wanted a name for their firm, but a name in itself was not enough – you needed the respect that went with it. The ICF inspired respect because they were the main firm, a firm others aspired to be like. For a period during the '80s they were number one, and everybody measured themselves against the ICF yardstick. Never before in the field of football violence had such a myth been built up around any football firm. They revelled in it, even appearing on a television documentary, earning the eulogies of female *Daily Mail* reviewers who admired their togetherness and family spirit.

Chelsea needed their own name and calling card and after one successful sorting out in the West End, someone picked up one of those freebie newspapers that are littered everywhere and noticed an advert for a group of corporate headhunters: 'That's what we are, headhunters, seeking out the main faces of rival firms.' From one-liners grow legends. The older fans were appalled by our descent into business card violence, but what did they know? They were still Ultravoxed out: dancing with tears in their eyes.

There has always been the feeling in youth culture that it might be over before you had the chance to participate in it. 'If only you'd been here last season. Now that was a real tear up.' Then they'd add that the away trip to so and so in '72, or was it '74, was so terrifying that they still got the jitters thinking about it, but there was always a pride behind the words, as if it had been the ultimate confrontation and nothing was ever going to better it. But the last punch-up was history. You were always looking forward to what was coming up.

———

Some Chelsea fans stood panting furiously, while others laid their exhausted bodies on the grass verge. Some stood around as though time were temporarily suspended. The police looked perplexed at the sudden immobility of everyone. It was the culmination of a fist-to-eyeball confrontation, a massive running

made you turn away from your pint and listen with a concentration so intense it would have seemed impossible a few seconds earlier, only to turn away glad that you didn't have that particular story in your memory bank.

Amongst that profundity, the press still offered up the old police infiltration tale to a willing public, because that's what they wanted to believe.

Not every Saturday was action-packed. As time went by, it became harder to have the mass battles of yesteryear and be fined a tenner on Monday morning. Confrontations had to be engineered, skilfully thought out like generals playing war games on Salisbury Plain. News of ambushes and brief encounters spread rapidly, single-clip bursts of frenetic energy, rat-a-tat-tat, then retreat into position. Battles were enacted in staccato bursts across concourses of shocked onlookers, who scattered or stood perplexed by the organised chaos, while police officers quickly regained control, but for what? All they did was re-establish the status quo while the battle continued somewhere else. Sometimes the police would turn up after the protagonists had disappeared and start pushing innocent people up against walls. You could see their frustration, especially the senior officers.

Every hooligan firm had their own league table listing who was the best. In the early '80s, the Arsenal boys started to make a big name for themselves (West Ham and Millwall didn't need to make names for themselves, they were the industry leaders). Denton had a tasty firm of old faces and dressers, while Miller had his little mob, the Herd, who were considered game. At the time, having a reputation as a game mob was about the highest compliment you could get. It was about turning up and being in the right place enough times to really make a difference and have a proper go when you could. Turning up, being seen to do the business and letting everybody know you were there and would make a difference because there was a huge difference between turning up to be seen and turning up and being seen to actually do something. Some of the mobs who came out of the woodwork would hide behind five rows of police, giving out massive verbal once inside the ground, surrounded by rows of reinforced metal, throwing coins, posturing, pretending they wanted to know: 'If it wasn't for the cops we'd do you lot,' they'd shout. Then 15 minutes before the end of the match, you'd see their bravado start to shrivel and then die. They would start edging closer to the police, waiting for an escort back to their train, nobody wanting to be at the back or front, then they'd get on their train and breathe a sigh of relief. Go back to their one-horse town to tell everybody how they fronted out Chelsea. Only those who turned up away from home not looking for Mr Plod's protection were considered to be in the top echelon.

Chelsea took trouble to the back yards of all the best mobs: Manchester United, Leeds, Manchester City, Everton and Cardiff. We were going to their cities and taking them on, drinking in their pubs, stopping outside their main boozers and offering them out, taking the piss. Manchester City took two maulings from us, which really brought it home to them that they hadn't yet arrived. A few of the boys, seeing an ace Evertonian face buying a kebab, sidled up to him in the shop and got him to purchase a few for the boys. Was that kebab a bit rich, or did he really shit his pants? In the full members' cup final at Wembley, every Chelsea nutter in England turned up. Manchester City Cool Cats quickly became lost cats then slippery cats, and slinked off in a coach which got trashed outside the Chalk Hill estate. Just a few local boys, nothing to do with the match, giving them one last send-off to tell them they'd been to London and it was paved with brick, so have it through the windows Manc. Yet still these mugs flooded the rumour factories with tales of how they'd done so-and-so. Hull City fans in Stockholm, telling how they'd slapped West Ham at Boothberry Park. Then six West Ham turned up and the Hull boys left a bit sharpish before you could say ICF.

Different bars became staging points, depending upon who was in town. Most mobs had their different entry points, apart from the beasts from the east who used to suddenly arrive where and when you'd least expect them.

Hickey would turn up at the small bar with the entrance on to

Sloane Square station, wearing his silly red beret and shades in the summer. Hickey, a man so far behind fashion he was ahead, was still always one step ahead of the game itself. Tinie's bar, ready for an intimate rumble, was how he put it.

Never more than 20 or 30 of us in the area, someone always hanging around outside checking out the people coming out of the station. This was the small-club haunt of Sheffield Wednesday and Derby, who'd give you a hard time up there, but only bring 200 and pretend they were Chelsea fans in and around the ground. Once people stopped wearing scarves it became easy for many fans to travel incognito with only local accents or geographical knowledge giving them away.

Without fail, there was always some silly little mob wanting to check out the King's Road. This pub afforded them an intimate Chelsea welcome, the personal touch of a verbal 'hello Mr Northern Bastard', then a smack in the teeth. Sometimes nobody showed and we'd just drink the time away, then catch a bus down the King's Road or drift further down to Riley's or the Drug Store. The real diehards who drank in the White Hart, packed shoulder to shoulder so that you were unable to lift your arm to get the pint to your lips sometimes, eschewed this novel approach to greeting away fans, but Hickey, our group, and a few others liked the personal touch.

When a small firm did appear they always hesitated and looked around, giving themselves away. The really confident mobs never hesitated for even a second. The doors would open and they would walk in as if they owned the whole world, arms swinging, full of confidence, with an inbuilt swagger. The northerners say that cockneys are born with it: swagger's disease, they used to call it. The door would open with a shout, 30 bandits opposite, then everybody would pile out, scattering the mob as the element of surprise always hit them. Then nobody would go there for a few weeks, leaving the police to sit outside with a full wagon-load of their finest bored witless. Someone always took the time to walk past and utter the immortal words in mocking tones: 'Expecting trouble, officers? There's rather a lot of you sitting there wasting taxpayers' money.'

And there was always another story about us filling the front and back pages of the papers, acres of forests felled to report our misdeeds: yet the young faces in the pictures couldn't possibly be capable of causing such mayhem and every picture stood time on its head, for there was always a distant look in the eye of someone who wasn't concentrating on the mayhem, but watching the match instead. It was possible to go to a match, which had been reported as being World War Three and be able to say, 'Trouble? I never saw any trouble.' Some Saturdays, during the pre-match drinking ritual, people would bring in clippings which sometimes stated the facts or more likely seemed bizarre. There was no one who didn't get a buzz from being famous in the tabloids for 15 minutes (until 15 minutes became 15 years' revenge), even if they poured scorn on some of the Ministry writings. Hickey came into the Black Bull one day, produced a clipping and read it out loud to his pals at the bar. Pretty soon the whole pub was listening. '"Fans on Warpath. Genoa, Italy: police arrested 34 football fans from Modena, northern Italy, after two petrol bombs, three marble 'cannonballs', flick knives, stilettos, swords, a scythe and four rocket guns were found on their coach on the way to Genoa stadium. Police said they were armed for a war." Now that's what I call tooled-up, boys. Food for thought everyone,' he boomed. The laughter reverberated around the pub for a short while, then everyone went back to their drinks and previous conversations.

People fell in love with the crowd scene and drinking rituals which football involved in a way normal people couldn't comprehend (although as we saw it, we were normal). Drink became our companion in arms, as if we couldn't hold a conversation about football without a pint glass in our hands and later a gram of sniff or whizz. The pubs around Chelsea and those who drank in them were our extended family, they became part of our psyche and where you drank, who you drank with and what you drank said a lot about you as a person. You were a White Harter, a Swan man or a Palmerston person. Some people flitted from pub to pub to catch the atmosphere and the gossip, which abounded in vast quantities. Others stood in the same spot they had always stood, frowning on those who couldn't remain static, as if relinquishing a space at the bar was akin to getting run on the terraces. Guys could manoeuvre a tray of eight pints through a space where nobody seemed able to move and not spill any. The buzz of laughter and chit-chat filled the air, swarming amongst the cigarette smoke with a life of its own, like the low residual hum of millions of bees. People stood in doorways holding conversations with anyone or no one, pontificating about how many would be coming down today. 'Villa, they'll have 40 at most. Coventry. Why bother leaving the pub?' Not that this is always the case.

There were other teams people got the big buzz on: Newcastle boys with bellies the size of a London semi-detached house, waddling past the pubs covered in scarves. Leeds fans pretending they were hard, yet walking with fear in every step. Tottenham, slipping in after mobbing up at some obscure pub in Kensington.

Hickey and the coach organisers moved around each pub selling seats at forthcoming away matches, able to glide effortlessly in and out of packed areas shaking hands and nodding, taking orders and money without disturbing the surface of the action. People would spot the coach ticket sellers, shout out their names, pay up and return to their pints. It was well ordered and regimented, which is amazing considering it was all done by word of mouth and a dozen telephone calls.

The Rose pub came to prominence and the Gunter Arms had its own little mob. A small group of faces would switch pubs and the new one would become the in-place. The punchers frowned on this. For them, being loyal to your Chelsea local was as important as standing your ground in a fight. The Imperial came into fashion. Somebody sprayed 'Hickey's Semi Men' on the wall outside. By now, Eccles's Elvis graffiti had been removed from Stamford Bridge. Nobody ever found out what 'Semi Men' meant. The dickhead who sprayed it never owned up, because it was obviously a mistake and he would have looked stupid and been ridiculed.

Football pub culture is such that people look up to someone

who can still run and fight after 12 pints, but overstep the mark, lose yourself in the bottom of a beer glass and all respect is gone. George Best must be the only exception to this. He played football at the highest level on a bottle of vodka a day. Even now, he can still pull top-class birds, despite being one step from the gutter.

Once, a solid guy, good drinker (he could stand his ground and still be able to do it after an all-day session), descended into a geezer who sat in the corner doing dozens of barley wine, missing the match to stay on the drink, then pissing his pants in the corner (okay, so we all laugh at stories of guys who go home slaughtered, stagger upstairs in the early hours and piss in their wardrobes with their missuses going berserk) because he couldn't make it to the toilet. He was faced with utter contempt from everybody. One day he walked out of the pub and fell in front of a car. 'Yeah, well, what do you expect when you miss the match and sit there pissing your pants?' everyone said.

———

Liverpool is a different country. Every Chelsea fan knows that. Even those Liverpudlians who live on the city's periphery talk about the city of Liverpool like it is another planet. Hadrian only built one wall, to keep the Jocks out. He should have built three. One in the original spot, then a second across the width of England around Watford to keep the northerners out of London and a third around Liverpool, like the M25 encircles London. The idea about the M25 wall was relayed to me by a group of Manchester City boys at an England match. They hate Liverpool with a venom that Londoners could never begin to understand, because we are too busy being in love with ourselves to get into a real hate game like that. The word is that certain employers will not employ people with certain Liverpool postcodes – and we're talking about northerners here. They hate London up there, even the police love to tell you how much they hate it, especially Chelsea. Get caught up there and they'd do you bad – nick your clothes, taxing they call it, then they cut you up just for the hell of it, for a laugh. Ha ha ha. A kicking or a slashing was an occupational hazard, but nicking another man's clothes was the lowest of the low. Every time Chelsea went up there, there were always young scallys hanging around eyeing up your trainers or shirts, looking to see if it was worth hanging around for the flotsam and jetsam if the fighters managed to cane you. 'Look out for Stanley', everyone used to say on the train, as if Stanley were a real person. He was really, he became a person as real as the bogeyman we feared as kids and could dole out severe disfigurement with one slash. You were always hearing horror stories about facial wounds – everybody was frightened of facial slashes – although you hardly ever saw anybody with a bad wound on their faces. To us, scouser and Stanley were one and the same. One of the lads baulked at that one day. Didn't like scousers being called Stanley, because he had an uncle called Stanley and he was a right nice geezer.

You had a sense of belonging, being a cockney in Liverpool, out of necessity more than anything else. Even loners wanted to mob together up there. There were dark skies everywhere, mirroring the looks you got and horribly echoing the dirt-covered buildings, never any sunshine. Get separated in Liverpool and there was always some little firm to catch you and ask you for the time and more. Woe betide you if you were wearing a Rolex, even a Bangkok moody was asking for extra rations of venom. Payback time, cockney, and that's for starters, for daring to show us you've got money here. Don't lose your bottle in Liverpool the older ones used to tell us, it's beyond the rhetoric of explanation, and you could tell they meant it, you could see it in their faces, in the fear reflected in their pints. It must have been frightening, because these were the people who were recognised as faces. When a top boy tells you he was losing it, you take notice. Chelsea always lose on the pitch up there which made it worse, although they never quite got the hang of the numbers we took up there or the liberties we dared to take on their turf. Playing in Liverpool, you're up against the worst that the city can throw at you, Everton and Liverpool. Sometimes I think they used to dredge the Mersey to really get some crap to throw at us. Scallywag scousers of popular myth, laughing and joking, cracking a stream of witty one-liners. 'Come ead,' they used to shout, or call us 'shite'. 'Learn to speak the Queen's English,' was our favourite wind-up when the insults started flying. We knew what they really wanted to give the cockney bastards: a 90-stitch stripe across the back.

They hung around Lime Street where the lights seemed to have a nasty sneering glare, goading you to cross the road, one hand down by their sides, moving their fingers, calling you forward. Thin-faced and gaunt with horrible sneers emphasised by that accent, always ready to run, or if the numbers were in their favour gloating at you, knowing they'd got you, then begging you to run to heighten the thrill of the chase, so that they could catch you and trip you into the gutter. Hoods up, one hand inside their silly anoraks, moving forward on their toes, arse up in the air. See cockney, we're tooled up and waiting. Look at us up on our toes dancing, while youse cockneys are all flat-footed and unsure. Then that horrible sound they uttered when they charged at you as one. A banshee of a sound. Anyone who heard it never wanted to hear it a second time. Once in retreat was enough for anybody.

'Wait here lads,' said Hickey one evening outside Lime Street, then took a small mob around the back and walked slowly up to them from behind. One silly scouser against a group of ten, bouncing up and down with his hand inside his coat. 'Come on, cockneys. Come ead.' Then silence. 'Check this out Stanley.' Whack, the sound of bare knuckle hitting just behind the ear, a drum bang crunch, the head straight onto the pavement because his hands couldn't break his fall. 'Feel free to stamp on his face at your leisure.' One last blink at the grinning cockney faces before the lights really went out. No one went home that night without feeling a sense of satisfaction. Years later you'd think that half of south London had stamped on him, so many people had related the story. When we went down there, there was always someone saying he'd had enough.

Get a small group in a pub and they are all scouse humour and 'Come on, Wack, we're only having a laugh', but see that group later when they're mob-handed by growling scousers and it's a different story. One group got told: 'You'll do well to call us Wack because that's what you're gonna get plenty of today.' Never met a scouse who didn't love to talk about how hard it is on the Scotland Road. 'Dare to walk down Scotland Road, cockney, and you'll be dead.' Hard men, hard drinkers. The more we heard, the more they sounded like a bunch of losers to us lot, pissed up in dirty, scruffy pubs. They talked to us about being hard, as if Londoners don't know about that.

On the bus to the ground, surrounded by ugly graffiti on the top deck, we felt superior to the people who lived in such filth and tolerated it. The graffiti wasn't the multicoloured, eye-catching graffiti art of New York City, it was an explosion of depression. Fuzzy Al, LFC Kop, Creggie Road Crew. Harsh painted names in black spray paint, reflecting their demeanour. The scousers seemed sneaky to us. Outside the ground the youngsters always tried to walk in amongst you, pretending they were only trying to be friendly. Where else do you have the police repeatedly telling you how treacherous the Liverpool streets can be? 'Keep moving, don't stand around here, it could be fatal,' the police would say outside Lime Street station. Then inside, 'Watch your step, cockney, you're one more stupid comment away from being ejected . . . and I wouldn't like to be in your shoes if that happens.' They were convinced that everybody was petrified of Clothes Horse Alley and Stanley-knife Park as they were known, until they met their nemesis in the Chelsea boys from the Battersea and Wandsworth high-rise ghettos, where even the rats trod lightly.

Now a police officer swaggered up the steps behind the Anfield Road stand, where a large group of the Chelsea lads sat together laughing and joking. His stick swayed from side to side. He looked more like Oscar Wilde trying to impress some young dandy fancy-man than the archetypal hard copper he wanted us to think he was. 'Keep the noise down you lot,' shouted the sergeant, pointing his brass-tipped stick at a group a few seats in. 'Don't come up here with your flash cockney mentality, because it's no bloody picnic, I'm telling you.' As if this stupid copper could convey the fear of his family and friends towards him to us. He couldn't even get close to our way of thinking. We thought we were superior because we came from London. In the lottery of English life, as Londoners we felt that we had won first prize. London had real villains like the Krays and Mad Frankie Fraser. Even Ronnie Biggs was more famous than any villain from Liverpool. What villains did they have? Militant leftie Derek 'Deggsy' Hatton, the scourge of Neil Kinnock, and Yosser Hughes going around slapping the nut on everybody. The Liverpool police eventually charged Derek Hatton with the theft of his own horse box. 'Fuck off,' we said to the copper, 'or we'll nick those stupid liver birds you've got up here and take them back to a real city.'

The copper looked perplexed that Chelsea were unfazed by his silly threats, then focused his ire on one fan who was sitting there smiling, the type of smile that is part deranged, part menacing, a manic half-smile which made the guy look as if he was about to burst into giggles. We could almost hear his thoughts as the crease lines in his brow cut ever deeper: why are you sitting there with that inane grin on your face? The more he thought about it, the more focused and angry his stare became. The fan's smile was all-knowing, as if daring the copper to ask him why he was smiling: if you ask me and I tell you you'll never dare to let your family out of your sight again.

'Have you got a problem, sonny?' asked the pig in an aggressive tone, after staring at him for another couple of minutes.

'Problem?' retorted the smiler with incredulity in his voice, 'We've got no worries, because we're the meanest geezers you've ever seen walking on your fucking streets.' Because that's what they were to him. His streets. They might have been filthy, rubbish strewn and covered in ugly abstract graffiti, but his Liverpool patch offered him respect far above anything he deserved, and here was Chelsea treating it with utter contempt. 'Do you want to get thrown out, you smart-mouthed cockney?'

'Do you mind? We're trying to watch a football match here.'

Then more laughter, because while the copper talked the talk, the lads knew that before the match they had walked the walk down Scotland Road and nobody had come near them. The Headhunters were now becoming mythbusters. 'You'll see, you just wait and see,' shouted the policeman, then walked away swinging his stick. At the end of the match the copper was the one smiling, because as usual, Chelsea had lost the match.

In the regular course of travelling, you had a lot of close calls. For example, the time we were on one of British Rail's finest carriages, travelling out of some hick town (they were always hick towns when you were leaving them) in the middle of nowhere. Crash. The bone-jarring sound of reinforced glass shattering, the higher density making the sound different to that of normal glass breaking, reverberated through the carriage. One minute we were all smiles, packs of cards and lads' banter, the next second we were sitting there covered in glass, with someone injured from a half brick or a lump of concrete. Angry shouts of 'dirty bastards' rang out, interspersed with people jumping back from the windows and looking for something to throw back, but all in vain as the gap-toothed half-wit with a demented expression was further back down the track doing another carriage, such was the momentum of the train. Shrill cries of 'you Chelsea wanker' or 'cockney bastard' pierced the air. The train driver jammed on the brakes so that those who had stood up to escape were doubly insulted by being hurled forwards by the sudden jolting stop of the train resulting in a heap of bodies and glass and everybody cursing their luck with foul expletives. Mostly, though, the damage was incurred by the rear coaches, as the first few coaches passed before the locals realised it was the Chelsea train. Those fortunate enough to be sitting in those coaches enjoyed a feeling of superiority, as those at the rear were at the mercy of the cold winds which blew in through the gaping windows and sat there trying to hold it together, while we walked back down the train with wide grins, consoling them for the discomfort they had to endure but smug in the knowledge that we could go back to our warm carriage. There's no honour in freezing your bollocks off. Memories of a kicking fade fast, but people still shiver at such horrible long trips back from the frozen wastelands of the north-east. This happened at both Newcastle and Sunderland on more than one occasion.

──────

Sometimes a train would stop in the middle of nowhere and everything would go quiet while all of us strained our ears for an announcement. If there was a problem with the train, then pretty soon the guard would come running through the train. Usually some idiot had pulled the communication cord, which was frowned upon because it meant more delays. One autumn on an outward journey from Euston, the cord got pulled three times before Nottingham and a few of the boys gave the cord-lovers a punch at Crewe station when the train arrived, while the BR guard looked on approvingly.

──────

Over a 20-year period, travelling football fans witnessed the decline and destruction of the industrial heartlands, even if they were completely indifferent to it. Where once huge factories and mills stood there were now barren waste grounds. The demolition teams gradually changed the backdrop and face of football. Many a time a half-demolished factory became a supply yard for a withering half-brick artillery barrage against fierce locals who became chastened and then terrified by the experience. The north-east was epitomised by this. One time some Chelsea boys, all designer trainers and tops, were met by a small Middlesbrough firm outside the station, immediately routed them and chased them across ground that was blackened beyond what a normal fire could do. Retracing their steps back to the main road, they noticed some black tar-like soot on their trainers. The police delighted in informing the lads that they'd never get it off and as a punchline told them that the ground had been declared a health hazard, unfit for human habitation. You could read the history of that wasteground just by looking at the red-black ash.

St James's Park, Newcastle, once a stadium where 55,000 throaty geordies roared their heads off (once, when Spurs played a League Cup semi-final second leg in the '70s, the noise was so loud and vibrant that the travelling Spurs fan who recounted the story started to shake as he remembered the fear and trepidation that that continuous rumbling roar of human noise had engendered in him) had now become a broken-down, ramshackle eyesore with only cobbled stone streets and rusty wharf crane jibs in memory of what had gone before.

The mighty Leazes' End, once the spiritual home of thousands of shipyard workers coming off their shifts, was demolished in the name of progress. In its place was put up a makeshift stand, held together with thousands of scaffold poles. The Newcastle fans traipsed to the Gallowgate end and were forced to endure seasons in the rain with no roof to echo their passion. A sad testament to the loyalty which typifies and echoes the history of north-east industrial relations. This is reality. It is only the sentimentality which comes with the perspective of time that makes us see it from a nostalgic viewpoint. Some of the guys look back and talk about the old terraces with more affection than the girlfriends whose names they have tattooed on their arms. The romance of the terraces. What romance? The team and the lads were our romance, everything else was pain and hardship. The blur of time wipes out frozen concrete wastelands, rusting iron girders, the endless waits and time killed waiting for the exciting parts. Standing alongside your mates in inclement weather seems romantic now, but the reality was icy winds suffered on cracked terraces, bone-chilling frosts coming up through your shoes until it felt like you had frostbite, winds that froze the fluid in your knee joints, disgusting toilets with no toilet paper (fans may have shat themselves with fear, but say you wanted a shit in an away end and you were looked at as being slightly mental), entrances and exits which were decrepit 40 years before.

When Lord Justice Taylor reported on football in the aftermath of Hillsborough, the decay that had been our travelling companion and constant bedfellow for 15 years shocked him. It also shocked the politicians, which showed how out of touch they really were. Music summed up the decay. 'Fog on the Tyne' sang the geordies, while the Londoners and Chelsea had Spandau Ballet with 'Gold'. 'Too Drunk to Fuck' by the Dead Kennedys was the reality of Newcastle.

Okay, so the meat pies up north were better, but the burgers were still the same, grease held together by fat. Perhaps only one person had the licence to produce these horrible things, as they were served up at every English football ground. If there really is anything in the BSE scare about cheap burgers and CJD, then there are a few hundred thousand football fans who will be top of the list, especially the obsessive food consumption beer monsters, who used to supplement their mega cholesterol intake with a double burger and onion ('go easy on the ketchup, mate, too much sugar is bad for you') pre-match, half-time and full-time snack. Burgers packed with so much colourant that they were pink.

'Two burgers to go, mate, plenty of onions. Any chance of a bread roll made this week, mate?'

A withering return glance was usually taken to mean no.

'Fuck off, dog's breath, I've got to sit next to you belching and farting for the whole return journey.'

'Stop moaning and get some sustenance down your neck.'

Then the souvenir to take home with them and down the pub the next day – the grease stain which always squirted out as you took a bite.

Sometimes the obligatory burger van was the recipient of

everybody's anger and was tipped over, which usually meant that the foodies moaned about being starving for the whole return journey. For many years, empty factories with smashed windows and bulldozed, burnt industrial wastelands adjacent to the pavement were home to rusty burger vans. These provided a perfect backdrop to the running battles that the Chelsea lads engaged the locals in. Later, much later, the industrial decay would be replaced by the glossy consumerism of retail (therapy) parks, but by then we'd become history as well.

———

Newcastle away games became a bit of a crusade for some Chelsea fans. Perhaps it stemmed from the fact that the London press always used them as a benchmark for the fans' loyal support, or perhaps it was because the geordies genuinely hated us. We had everything they despised, especially jobs and money, and we were flash with it. The silly buggers talked about Byker estate as if we should be impressed by it. It was an ugly monstrosity which rose like a misshapen pyramid, as if a geordie designer had vomited on bricks and had a vision of a new housing estate. When the building game was at its peak in the housing boom of the '80s some lads would go away with a serious wedge in their pockets, pulling it out in a northern pub and flashing the cash big time.

At the time, the half-caste Gary from Middleton was reckoned to be the Newcastle top boy. He was in a firm called the Gremlins. This firm was supposed to be up for it, but from what we could gather their main claim to fame was sitting in the café opposite the main railway station and boxing out a few early arrivals who wanted a nice fried breakfast at 10 a.m. Slapping a few fanzine writers who liked a serious fry-up was not where Chelsea was at.

Not only did the lads down south have all the jobs, but their work often meant that they were sent up to the north-east during the week, giving it the big one on site before flying back on a

Friday evening. This meant that we knew the boozers where the major geordie firms hung out. One year, Chelsea fans got bricked all the way back to the train station and in revenge Chelsea targeted their main boozer. The Newcastle mob outside The Strawberry stood no chance and ran off while a tidy Chelsea mob put in their windows. The geordies inside were shitting themselves, lying on the floor holding their arms or tables over their heads. Carlo handed out potatoes for the lads to play at target practice with Spud-U-Like geordie.

Ginger Terry was there that day and he recorded it for posterity in his diary. At his trial, it was quoted and reported in every newspaper in the land: 'Done a pub load of geordies . . . We done well against the geordies, they were terrified.' After the match, they had upped the ante, showering everybody with bricks and bottles indiscriminately and attacking every small group of Chelsea fans they could find. They then spent the next 12 months putting it about that they were going to take revenge, and would take a big shit on Chelsea's main firm if they ever dared to go near the top boy's boozer, The Farmers' Rest.

The next season, a few Newcastle boys took a giant liberty by walking into the main Chelsea pubs offering out fans on a one-to-one basis (the romantic bastards, they really thought they were film stars), so at the return fixture the Chelsea mob taught the geordies a lesson outside the pub. Others upped the ante even higher by introducing the geordies to a surgeon's knife. It was a moment they'd collectively never forget. One of the victims was still having nightmares two and a half years later. The press quoted him: 'I used to get nightmares quite often. I was reliving what happened. I still get them now and then, but I've recovered from the attack now.'

Walking away from the devastated Strawberry, the lads gave themselves a round of applause. The police, though, had other ideas and they caught about 50 of us near the ground, then shepherded us into a car park where they kept us for the whole match. To add insult to injury it was drizzling, that horrible fine stuff guaranteed to soak right through your designer threads.

The geordie weather was punishing us in a way that the fans couldn't. Once the match was over and we were deposited on the train out of town, though, the humour came back as the steam rose from our warming bodies.

York Road meant the York Tavern, a favourite hangout for the Wandsworth boys. Battersea Bob drank in there. He was well known in the York, and his fame spread to Chelsea for ram-raiding off-licences during the Brixton inner-city riots. 'Those blacks are bombing the police while I'm out earning,' he said. People reckoned he had so much drink stashed in his flat next to the River Thames that he almost had a subsidence problem.

Nowadays the York Tavern is a smart-looking office, but in the '70s and '80s it was a Chelsea stronghold. All the coaches used to drive along that road and after the match they would inch their way through the traffic jams heading back to the motorway. In 1984, the Friday night before Chelsea played Newcastle, some lads finished working on the building sites early and stashed all their debris plus some traffic cones in the middle of the Wandsworth Bridge roundabout. On the Saturday after the match, a few of the Battersea lads used the cones to narrow the road, making the traffic jam even worse and setting up an ambush. Three Newcastle coaches came past the York and gave the usual V signs and verbal abuse to those drinking inside. A little further down the road, the ambush came and the lads used all the ammunition they had stored the previous day to smash every window in the coaches. It took five minutes for the police to arrive, such was the traffic chaos caused by the cones. By then, everybody had disappeared leaving metal frames with no windows for coaches and shell-shocked passengers.

Even better, Gary and the Newcastle Gremlins had come down and were also ambushed at West Brompton. As the doors opened, Gary was greeted with a fire-bucket full of sand in the face. It was an old Indian trick – I saw it in an Audie Murphy western, but we included a bit that wasn't in it. Those who were holding their eyes were battered about the heads with the empty fire-buckets. Fat Pat was actually squirting a Jif Lemon in people's faces. He reckoned later it was ammonia, but the general feeling was that it had only contained lemon. Our firm thought Fat Pat was okay, although some didn't have much time for him, as he seemed to spend too much time talking about violence and setting up rows and not enough actually getting stuck in when it happened, but you had to accept that having a go at him alone meant that he might get the big squeeze on you. Our lot never trusted anyone who seemed able to converse with other firms about setting up a row.

There were grounds where the locals lived for the 90 minutes of football, then turned their ire at having lost on the travelling cockneys as if it were a compulsory sport. See you for tea mum, after I've settled a few regional scores with those London chappies. Seeing their massed ranks in the tight terraced streets always dissipated any feelings of cockiness that the Chelsea fans had. Whilst they might have been mobbed up, numbers never really meant much if you were organised. But it didn't matter how many times you ran then, some mobs would still be waiting for you. They seemed to see it almost as a ritual sacrifice but nobody was going to die, we weren't Roman gladiators and there was no honour in defeat. Hemingway wrote *Death in the Afternoon* to describe the magnificent spectacle of the bullfight and the tragic finale of the slaying of the bull. For us, defeat meant 1–0 and being forced onto your toes by a rival firm. People didn't salute or applaud your actions. There was no '*Olé*' for us, though they might have given a grudging respect. Spectacle, colour and blood. Hemingway would have loved it, he would probably have wanted a part of what we had, such was his desire for a thrill. In a way our rituals mirrored those of the bullfight, with all the parading and posturing that went on. Fighting around a spin of the dice, which for the most part was fun combined with pure aggression, depending on the numbers that showed. We didn't have to be what people wanted us to be, pure and simple. Add the coexistence of brutality and respect, solitude and comradeship, cowardice and courage, and you have the whole picture.

Stories abounded about people having one-on-one straighteners. Babs being offered out by West Ham's top boy outside the Britannia. Dave Smith from Arsenal going up to Middlesbrough and knocking out the main face in the Incognito Club, hitting him so hard with one punch that his legs buckled like a new-born giraffe, making the locals think he was doing the funky chicken. But one-on-one fights weren't what it was about. The group mentality was what made it all tick, our allegiance to the creed of belonging and being part of a fighting group. What went before the charge and the contact was often better than the contact itself. The exhilaration of anticipation of the match and everything else that surrounded it was what it was all about.

Not wanting to fight at football seemed unnatural, almost un-British. Being a part of the football crowd was our replacement for childhood memories of picnics in the park with 'Tizer the appetizer' or Sunday lunch listening to *Two-way Family Favourites*. These people were our family and we were close to them in a way the average person on the street couldn't comprehend. We were intimate in a non-intimate sort of way. Mates who knew more about each other than their wives, girlfriends or parents would ever know. And more than that we understood each other. People talked about taking on rival groups, using the collective 'we'. Belonging to the group and the team was a way of life. In football violence you were part of a group, yet in reality there were only two men, yourself and the person you were whacking. It was necessary to choose your team and group allegiance wisely, because hardly anyone ever changed teams, only leaving with retirement. It was better to be an absent face than have no credibility.

Running when it came to the crunch was the end. Even if the lad who ran redeemed himself a thousand-fold over the years his nickname, which would usually be allied to that of a famous runner – Kip Keno Hughes, or Harris did a Viren (after the famous Olympic athlete Lassie Viren) – stuck. It was as if nicknames associated with acts of cowardice were superglued on. Nicknames were almost a religion in London. Everybody had a nickname, but nobody seemed to know how they came about. Untold, Scat Man, Skitzy, Merve the Swerve, are all examples of people who were known only by their nicknames. When Chelsea mates telephoned them at home, their mums answered and often put the telephone down with the words: 'Nobody of that name lives here.' Pete Davis picked up the name 'Shooter'. Those who didn't know him thought it was because he had actually used a gun, but in fact it was because everywhere he went, he informed us that this firm or that one carried shooters. Also, every story he ever told had a shooting in it somewhere.

'Bristol City away next week, Peter.'

'Dodgy place, bad area that St Paul's, they're shooter merchants they are, mate,' he'd say solemnly while others tried not to laugh. Every time he said the word, people would put their arms inside their jackets as if they were pulling a gun. Cops-and-robbers games in the playground had transformed into something tangible in Shooter's imagination.

Stories did the rounds about people changing allegiance because they wanted a better row, but these people were either cowards who only wanted to mingle with the hardest firms or one step away from the nuthouse. Daft Donald was a bit short upstairs and professed to support everybody. He had tattoos on his arm reading 'West Ham', 'Man U' and 'Chelsea'. He even had 'Road Rats' tattooed on his lip. That was one firm who didn't want interlopers, especially some punk-music-loving half-wit. One night, four Road Rats descended on the King's Road with the intention of cutting the tattoo out. Luckily for Donald, he was supporting someone else that night. After that he stuck to football and kept away from the King's Road.

Standing behind a row of police gave plenty of idiots bravery far beyond their normal limits. Then the spit would fly from them. Spittle on your face is the worst feeling in the world. You wipe it off as fast as you can, not wanting it to dry. If it does dry, you seem unable to get the smell of the other person's spittle out of your nostrils until the next day.

Everyone was fearless in their time. Fear was nowhere, even

when it surrounded you like a dense jungle. But when it hit you, the fear came like a blade cutting into your insides and turning your legs to jelly, especially when there was nowhere to run or hide. What we felt wasn't the fear of getting hurt: it was something beyond that, more intangible, which made the pursuit of what we were looking for even more exquisite. Some guys spent a whole week crapping their pants about a trip somewhere and spent the whole match being nearly sick with fear then returned home to tell everyone what a great time they'd had and how they'd been looking forward to it all week. Then they would go through exactly the same ritual again the next week. They must have been praying for the close season, only to miss those feelings of terror. Getting knocked out in front of everyone was instant, but to suffer the degradation of being seen to run in terror in front of thousands of others was real and complete humiliation. The hardest guys would stand and tell others that if they ran, they would have to answer to them. They would nod in terror, then get on their toes at the first sight of a rival firm though afterwards they'd deny point blank that they had ever run in their life.

Fear, like pain, is relative, but the worst kind is group fear, when everyone senses that it is about to come on top. Idiots mumbling the mantra of the defeated: 'It's bad, it's really bad', and looking around imploring others not to run; 'stand there' in their eyes. When it really came on top, you looked at the people around you to see if they were as scared as you. If they looked like they weren't, you hoped they were insane and that they might be the lone ranger saviour, copping it for the greater good, so that you could laugh about the escape and his bruises in the pub. If they did look scared, it made you feel a lot worse. There were people who lost it completely and shit in their underpants, real shit that you could smell, not just a metaphorical accusation of 'shitting yourself'. They were never seen again.

Our experiences were spiritual as well as physical. I've seen guys who couldn't knock the skin off a rice pudding take unbelievable punishment, staying on their feet as if they had strings holding them up. It was possible to feel uplifted by a beating, as if you'd received a rite of passage. People discovered strength and courage – some even performed better after they'd been hurt a bit: 'Shit, mate, I discovered pain out there and it felt good.'

Sometimes you needed help, though, and it could come in the shape of mates or the Old Bill, or best of all a nutter who'd charge in and turn the tide – one solitary figure standing in the middle of the road, hundreds facing him, holding them up with the immortal words, 'Who wants it, then?' Every individual coming at him had to think whether they really did want it with this lunatic, before somebody accepted and the nutter copped it.

A kicking, or a hiding as we liked to call it, was nothing of the sort really, but rather a mass exchange between hundreds. Even those who went down and stayed down for some considerable time usually got up and lived to fight another day. Often a blow hit you and you rode it out, because the adrenaline rush was so great that the endorphins flowing meant that the pain didn't feel real. Afterwards, over a pint, you felt good that you'd taken a good hit and kept going. It gave you credibility and you could declare that somebody else who had been sparked out was a wanker with a glass jaw. Sometimes people would punch for show, a half-punch, just to establish a pecking order, to put someone in their place, sometimes it could be a nasty uppercut. Once I saw someone out cold being run at and kicked by a group of four or five guys. These were deliberate kicks – they aimed their boots at the spots they wanted to hit; chest, legs, back. The police later stated that the guy had 95 per cent bruising on his upper body.

Sometimes someone would get laid out with a blow of crisp simplicity executed with precision, but mostly you could ride the blows out and only suffer stiffness and bruising the next day. Trying to drink a pint a few days later with a mouthful of ulcers where the cuts are healing, with your mates laughing at you, is no joke though.

For most, fear passed as fast as it had arrived and became a good-time memory, like a horror movie where people are petrified yet come out of the cinema laughing. A whole day might be spent being attacked and assaulted, but you could still wake up on a Sunday morning with a spring in your step. Stories became legends during a two-hour drinking session, in the space between one match and the next. Bruises became badges of honour, lost teeth became a permanent reminder, while stab and slash wounds (not facial ones mind you) were shown off in much the same way as children compare appendix scars.

Much worse than anything that actually happened to you was the dread of what might be to come. This wasn't helped by the old-timers who would say, shaking their heads, 'one day, son, you're gonna cop it real bad', or 'there's a nasty firm out there waiting for you'. For some this came true. For most, the mob mentality made it possible to have fun in a group and then poodle off home.

'MUFC KICK TO KILL' they sprayed, but nobody took it seriously. Seeing a mob who lived up to their graffiti and really did kick to kill was unusual. Millwall kicked to kill and scousers slashed to scar, but you didn't need graffiti to tell you that. Everyone knew who the most terrifying firms were and measured their cloth accordingly. If you were going somewhere which was perceived as grim, then the noise level dropped as the anticipation rose. Getting hurt badly was something that happened to someone else, and after a while the stories about somebody really copping it were pooh-poohed so often, when the victim walked into the pub with a few scratches and bruises, that these tales floated away on a wave of incredulous shaking heads.

———

Then it happened. Death touched you more than anybody cared to admit, especially when it was someone you knew. Aeroplanes dropped out of the sky, but they were just statistics on the news. When it was one of your own it hurt. When Gary Lee was killed at Preston, a part of everyone died at Chelsea that day. The press reported that he was chased into a multi-storey car park, fell off a wall while trying to escape and died from his injuries. Everybody had at least one story of a chase to tell, and were usually able to include a humorous escape ending. Gary Lee's ending was without any humour. People said that they would stop going as a mark of respect, in the same way that the death of a comrade in war makes talk of peace fill the air. But the next Saturday, his death became just another statistic, nothing personal. Everyone remembered and then got back to business, waiting for the day when Chelsea played Preston again.

In a world where lunatics were treated worse than animals, the so-called nutter had real respect within football crowds. 'He's a nutter' was a term of affection. It raised people's profiles and standing, because it meant a lack of fear of bodily harm. Even the hardest were afraid of real injuries, but nutters thrived on it, so their rapid evolution up the pecking order was ensured. After receiving such a kicking, nutters would sometimes come into the pub with their heads swollen to what seemed like twice the size and that was after three days in hospital! As some wag would always point out to the rest of the pub, there was no chance of brain damage because there was usually a distinct lack of brain to begin with.

THE MUSIC REVOLUTION

THE SHED END IN THE LATE '60S AND EARLY '70S was skinhead city, Paki-haters every one. They embraced the politics of the far right, yet listened to black music and claimed the rhythms as their own. The Skinhead Moonstomp, Harry J and The Allstars played classic reggae tunes which were later to be immortalised on the *Tighten Up* volumes. Then there were the harsher dance tunes of ska music, epitomised by the rude boys from Jamaica. Feared and reviled by the society that had created them, the skinheads would retreat to the public bar before going on to a club and listening to their beloved dance music. Then the skinheads grew their hair and the sounds moved into Tamla and the sound of Philadelphia, but whatever the rhythms from the records or the new fashions dictated, some of the lads stayed true to their skinhead roots and their love of Chelsea remained intact. Music and football were inseparable in those days, as they are today.

The massed terraces of skinheads transformed themselves in the time it took to grow their hair and shave sideburns. Skinhead to suedehead, the change was accompanied by an ever-present musical soundtrack. 'So I'd Like to Know Where You Got the Notion' by the Hues Corporation was the anthem of the early, '70s, that time of transformation. But although the trends changed three times in a decade, the attachment of fashion to football and vice-versa didn't. The right-wing skinheads stayed true to their roots and the diehards were still the same. And through the metamorphoses of skinheads to punks back to skins one truism never changed with the hairstyles: white working-class youth loved football and England.

Friday night was beer night long before the marketing men thrust lager into the English consciousness. Since the Industrial Revolution, men and beer have been inseparable on pay-day, arriving at their locals and chucking it down their necks so that they have to loosen their belts, ordering a few more just before the bell declares chucking-out time at 11 p.m. and cries of 'Time, gentlemen, please' are heard all over England from throaty, rotund landlords or their feisty wives. The doors open, and men spill out laughing and joking.

'Going home to give the wife one, then?'

'Leave it out, it ain't Christmas, is it?'

These one-liners are repeated again and again as England gets set for a cholesterol-slammer supper of late-night fish and chips, pickled gherkins or, better still, a greasy kebab or a Ruby Murray. Alcohol really kicks in hunger, after eight pints of liquid fizz, making you crave belly-swelling food that will sit on the stomach until the fry-up the next morning and ensuring that the middle-aged belly strains against the shirt buttons. Hearing these people, and the rest of middle England, resting their bellies on the bar while mocking punks was something football fans knew all about.

Youth have always looked upon the older generation with disdain and punk was the vociferous voice of the new revolution. Like the football terraces, it was going to change England as we knew it. It was the music of violence and revolution, and it permeated every facet of society because of the dearth of new sounds.

Punk thrust music to the forefront and its violent dancing and attitude competed with football hooliganism for the front pages. The inhabitants of King's Road on Saturdays in 1976 dressed for the part in spiky hair, bondage trousers, Doc Marten boots and clothes ripped and held together by safety pins for no other reason than to shock. They drank pints of snakebite – lager and cider – too quickly, then chucked up. Pubs that didn't want us put signs on their doorways, snakebite not sold here, or when you got inside they would say: 'We don't serve your type or that sort of drink.' No, but they'd serve someone a triple whisky to make sure they got 32 measures out of every bottle, wouldn't they? The surge of 1950s Teddy Boys and the '60s summer of love were replaced by punk.

The year 1974 was dubbed the 'Year of the Cover Version' by Johnny Walker on Radio 1. Apart from the soul boys listening to the sounds of Detroit, Philadelphia and Harlem, what original music was coming out of England? Punk had arrived, and it centred around Chelsea. Skinheads and soul boys watched punk music take the centre stage of fashion and it dictated youth culture. Punks were described as more shocking than football fans; listening to music, sniffing the mood and the glue was where it was at. That whiff of formaldehyde and the glazed-eye stagger of the glue boy were unmistakable. Lady Esquire shoe colouring in your dad's best monogrammed hankie.

Chelsea boys went to football matches alongside the punks. We'd jump up and down on the terrace after a goal and later while doing the Pogo in a club. Sweaty bodies pushed up against each other, and later we would spit over the person next to us and the band. Lead singers would stand there covered in white phlegm.

Saturday afternoons, the lads spitting at their rival fans across a divide of metal or coppers. White Riot. Riot riot, we want a riot. Heysel was eight long years away. So far in the distance that the Ministry couldn't even contemplate it.

Football hooligans didn't have a monopoly on terrorising people. Punks were so frightened they'd miss the boat on reinventing youth culture that they marched every Saturday, despite the policemen telling them that they couldn't walk up and down the King's Road. The Chelsea Drugstore put a whole new slant on the name of the pub. E culture was yet to happen but shock culture was about to explode into the nation's living-rooms.

Bill Grundy, the dirty old man, leered at the punk bird sitting in his television studio. 'Go on, then, say something outrageous,' he goaded. 'Fuck off. Bollocks, you wanker,' she obliged. The Ministry were shocked, told us that the punks had been drinking alcohol before they'd been allowed on ITV at 6 p.m. In the ensuing public outrage, ITV sacked Bill Grundy. People feared that children would be corrupted by the sight of Johnny Rotten with his spiky hair and green teeth and predicted that Rotten and his ilk were the beginning of the end of the English-speaking peoples. EMI sacked them from their record label. Dance halls up and down the country lined up to ban the Sex Pistols, which wasn't perhaps a bad thing, because rumour had it that they couldn't play their instruments properly. Another record company signed them up and they went to number one in the charts, even though Radio 1 had banned them. Girls wore make-up that made them look like Alice Cooper, who sang 'School's Out' and bit the heads off chickens. The Ministry reported that he'd had a rabies scare after biting the head off a rat.

Who cared about anything when you had punk? Now, the boys would smash up a pub to the sound of The Clash or Generation X, instead of The Four Tops.

The Ministry was absolutely appalled at what was happening in England. For a short time it seemed completely out of control. Headlines screaming 'Day of Shame', 'Soccer's Animals', and 'Big Match Uproar' filled the front and back pages. 'God Save the Queen' hit the top of the charts. People out there were getting very frightened.

Cheeky Pete's disco, Brolly's next door and below it the Bier Keller, down by the River Thames, had seen nothing like it. On a Thursday evening, four punk girls disturbed the calm of the disco, laughing at the ageing soul boys in their flared peg trousers and bowling tops: Top Man fashions. They stood there in bin liners, black stockings and suspenders, with white bleached spiky hair. Others had bleached jeans and safety pins holding together rips in almost every part of their clothing. This was an eye opener to the locals. After the first shock which greeted everyone when they met their first punk, the clubs sprang from nowhere.

The World's End market sold the fashions, if you could call them that, while pubs such as The Roebuck on Lower King's Road catered to the requirements of the new revolutionaries. Punks and skins mingled in together, oblivious to their supposedly opposing cultures. Soul boys turned up to fight both of them, a sport which replaced the Paki bashing of old. Teddy boys stood at the door selling blues at three for £1: uppers which would keep you going all night in a mad dance frenzy, then downers to bring you back to the reality of Monday morning.

In the early days anybody could become a star, but as time went on punk went the way of all youth culture, with recognised faces emerging. In The Roebuck, Siouxsie Sioux of Siouxsie and the Banshees held court at the bar. The Damned stood there swearing with the best of them. Their time was to come later when like all the rest they sold out. Their biggest hit came from a remake of 'Eloise', but for now they enjoyed the buzz that punk brought.

The punk scene was likened to that of the football terraces in the early '70s, when it was brash and fresh and really shocked the masses. Punks and football fans were living in a parallel world. We were both shocking society to the core, giving it a collective V sign, but any thoughts that the two trends would come together in a seductive embrace were firmly scotched when a punk ventured into the Chelsea north stand in 1977, for the match against Ipswich. Wearing a Sex Pistols 'God Save the Queen' T-shirt and a black donkey jacket with the words 'White Riot' on the back, he encountered nationalists. 'Oy, you wanker, you're against the Queen,' then a kick up the arse followed by flailing fists as retribution was dished out on behalf of the Queen.

When the police rescued him, they ejected him from the ground and informed him that punks were trash and that should he try and enter the ground wearing a nappy pin again, he would be arrested for carrying an offensive weapon.

The Roxy club at Convent Garden had black walls and warm beer in plastic glasses, but what the hell, it shut at 2 a.m. and any new fashion was where it was at. The punk music scene was about a new revolution. In the Roxy, they were catering for music lovers.

Thursday became poofs' night out: 'handbag night' to real men. The Vortex on Wednesday nights: another basement club where the acoustic feedback from debut bands almost burst your eardrums. The fanzine *Sniffin' Glue* started life here. The Marquee club, all darkness inside, then up a slope to the tightly packed dancefloor. Bar lights glowed at the back, next to an emergency exit, where lads used to slip in as our fathers did to picture houses in the '50s.

In the London clubs, the fashion of football was reflected in the laconic slouches of those listening to the lyrics and supporting the bands.

During the punk years, the press reported every violent incident at a game almost as though it were a prelude to the complete breakdown of law and order. The lads fought on a Saturday afternoon, and the new punk bands sang about it later in their raw, unrefined lyrics.

As soon as it was here, punk was gone. The end was near on New Year's Eve 1979, when Johnny Rotten, with his group Public Image, stood on stage laughing at the paying public. He didn't want anybody spitting at him. Billy Idol sold out and accepted lucrative record contracts. Even Madness went the same way, and became more interested in Top Ten hits and their image than in really playing the music.

Punk had lived and died. It was up to the football boys to take over once again.

The terraces were the alter-ego of popular music. The term rock and roll was outdated American slang, while punk bands gave voice to the actions of football fans, but football lasts for only 90 minutes and the music followed the swift ending of the match. Every group had their own following and punks showed how quickly fashions changed. Watching bands became an extension of going to an away match.

The group Madness were an embodiment of all we wanted to be. They had great dance tunes, silly dancing and feel-good lyrics, going to the top of the charts with rewrites of the old ska stuff. Seeing them on stage, we felt like it could have been any of us. Graham McPherson, better known as Suggs, was reputed to have travelled on Hickey's coaches. 'Madness, they call it madness' was a line from one of their biggest hits. It summed up the mood of the time exactly. Madness played at Coventry in the 1979–80 season. Their concerts were more like an away football crowd than a music crowd, all noise and chanting with no niceties. It was also a territorial thing with the Coventry blacks, who followed the Specials, taking a dislike to a mob of London boys turning up. In the days before the word 'dissing' (to disrespect) entered the language of the street, that was exactly what we were doing. The atmosphere got more tense with every song, so that you couldn't even watch the band or go to the bar. All you could do was stand your ground and wait.

Eventually a shout went up of 'Get the cockneys', then a rumble and crush of bodies going forward, mingled with the screams of girls, the sound of bodies hitting the floor and the muffled thud of flesh on flesh as the London boys were steamed by the Coventry. Foxy from Battersea, Chelsea fan Mark Self and I tried to hold the door shut against the braying lunatic mob. Three pairs of hands were all that stood between us and a fate that didn't bear thinking about.

When the West Ham lads went to Birmingham to see the Cockney Rejects, it was an away game in its own right. The night that the Cockney Rejects played at Birmingham has long since passed into legend. West Ham battled it out with Brummie

United to the Bubbles theme tune. The football and music mobs became inseparable, and West Ham doing the security for the Rejects took the mind back to the Hell's Angels working for the Rolling Stones – in those days their brand of security meant that stepping out of line warranted a beating with pool cues. Perhaps unsurprisingly, people took advantage of the fact that terrace scores could be settled away from the rows of uniformed bobbies and mounted police at the matches. One Saturday night at the Electric Ballroom in Camden Town was symptomatic of what was happening everywhere: the Gooners waited for West Ham outside, while the police remained oblivious. While the national press wrote lurid headlines about the football terraces the music press, in the form of *Sounds* and *New Musical Express*, wrote about the very real violence at music concerts the length and breadth of England.

At the Electric Ballroom in Camden Town in the '80s, roller-skating came back into fashion. The queue streched right around the corner. Red Beans & Rice, Bad Manners and Madness were headlining. For everybody who was there (except Red Beans & Rice, who got bombed off the stage by a barrage of bottles and cans, full and empty), it was generally thought to be one of the defining concerts of the era.

The bouncers wanted all swastika armbands removed because it would cause problems with future licensing, but the scene was set for a musical extravaganza. Buster Bloodvessel did the can-can on stage while the boys danced.

Gone were the flared trousers, wedge shoes and Oxford Bags which had epitomised the '70s. Looking at pictures of the old puncher brigade running across a pitch with 30-inch flares on, or putting the boot in with a seven-inch heel, it was no wonder that people couldn't take youth culture seriously.

The audience that night were soul boys, every one of them, the direct descendants of the skinhead era. From Trojan Records, the Pioneers with 'Let Your Yeah Be Yeah', via Desmond Dekker's band The Israelites to the Motown sound, football and music became interwoven at every juncture. Steve Walsh, an ageing

Radio London DJ has-been, made a huge comeback by taking a football chant and transferring it to the dance floor, then bringing out a record, over-dubbing the fatback band's 'I've Found Loving' with a terrace chant to produce 'You What?'

With his sidekick, the self-confessed football-hater Tony Blackburn, they chanted it across the tannoy until the dancefloor resembled the Shed, the Shelf or Northbank, with the DJ chanting and the crowd chanting back as one. One night in the Lyceum, it went a stage further when the Arsenal and Tottenham boys took 'You What?' across the dancefloor, then outside and across Waterloo Bridge in a massive battle which the police seemed powerless to control.

Mickey Dread, the bass player in Culture Club, was a Chelsea fan. The day they did the video at Chelsea, Boy George, the fat poof, took untold stick. The Chelsea boys might have enjoyed music but found that being backdrop for a gay songster was a bridge too far.

Sham 69 enjoyed the biggest skinhead following. They liked to go on stage with the British Movement Party leader guard around them. Jimmy Percy must have seen it as a fashion thing, but the BMP guys saw it as something more.

Skinheads went right-wing again in the late '70s. Some skins stayed true, but most changed their allegiances and fashions many times in those ten years. Their music wasn't that great, but for a while it was good to follow Sham 69. On the wall of the Kingston Coronation baths, an advert for wearing seatbelts was up for a while. Clunk Click said its caption, beneath a picture of a female face after going through a car windscreen. 'You too can have a face like mine' the caption went on to say, hoping to shock us. 'Yeah, at the next Sham 69 concert,' sprayed a wag.

I remember McGregor, the QPR fan, 5ft 2ins tall, with longish light-brown hair and a gold tooth, a lairy little swagger about him. He was a cocky little basard from Ladbroke Grove who aligned himself with every team. The first time I ever saw him was in 1979, when Madness played the Acklam Hall club under the Westway. He walked through it in a Gabbici top looking around at all the Arsenal boys as if he held some sort of sway with them, the Jimmy Cagney of west London staring everybody out. The whole of Ladbroke Grove turned out that night because they thought there was a crowd of east London skins coming down. McGregor left and a huge mob tried to break in and some belligerent blacks starting lobbing firebombs. And the band played on.

Madness were known as the 'North London Nutty Boys' and one of their biggest fans was Fat John from Paddington, who was known as Prince Nutty. He appeared on the first Madness video doing the nutty dance.

Demarcation lines were drawn around the fans of different bands, just like they were drawn around opposing football fans two hours after a match. Young men tested the mettle of their counterparts and then retreated back into real life. On building sites on Monday mornings people who'd been separated the previous Saturday by a thin blue police line laid bricks alongside each other.

West Ham were their usual territorial selves and watching boxing at York Hall in Bethnal Green became a no-go, as they made it known that turning up mob-handed to support another boxer would be seen as an invasion. Years later when Mark Kaylor, who used to fight in West Ham colours, came up against Tony Sibson, the darling of Leicester, the two sets of fans continued their terrace rivalry in the boxing arena. The one-liner from the famous boxing commentator Reg Gutteridge went down in history: 'There's more fighting outside the ring than in it,' he barked as chairs and bottles landed around his head. Surprisingly, the Leicester followers of Sibson were harder than those who followed Leicester City; aptly called, by themselves, the Baby Squad.

From the remains of punk came the hard-edged guitar sound. One night in a Fulham punk club, some people came in wearing swastika armbands. It had instant shock value. Around the same time skinheads made a comeback. The combination of raw lyrics, aggressive music and swastika armband fashion saw the emergence of right-wing music. There were plenty looking to get in on that scene. After all, they thought to themselves, why not have skinhead bands representing all that's best in the white working class? In America, Bruce Springsteen had depicted the destruction of white working-class steel communities in hard-edged lyrics which turned economic hardship and misery into the profits of the music industry, so why not here too? Songs were coming from people who were the same as you. The music scene change was ripe for it, because we couldn't relate to the groups anymore. People floated around London dressed as New Romantics, but worse was to follow. Seeing everyone in the Black Bull singing along to the lyrics of the Tom Robinson song 'Glad to be Gay' was more than we could bear. 'Shit,' said Hickey, 'I can remember when gay meant happy.'

Screwdriver led the way with their fierce lyrics and '70s skinhead look. Only the hard-core extremists cared about the lyrics: for everybody else, the music and the fact that it was played by skinheads was where it was at. Part of the cult following was into what skinheads represented, while for others it was just another fashion statement. Hanging around with skinheads who were diehard white, working class and Chelsea, I joined in forming the band Combat 84. Its original ethos was based on our combat dress and George Orwell's *1984* but others saw the group as some form of racist splinter group. Everybody who was a skinhead was suspected of being a racist, but that's no nearer the truth than saying that every English person is a white supremacist. In fact, we weren't political, just a simple four-piece band with me as lead singer and lyricist. I just wanted to say something about life through music. On lead guitar was Ji Johnston, Depford John Armitage played the bass, and Brownie on drums. We'd all earned the right to be a band through having worked as roadies and had been thrown off the Go Gos' tour for touching up one of the backing singers. Belinda Carlisle, the lead singer, later to become very big, didn't like our football fan attitude either.

'When you're on your knees with a gun to your head it's better to be dead than fucking red': what else would a right-wing leaning skinhead band write about? In football you'd always want to play the big stadiums, yet the best grounds are those with smaller gates but better atmospheres. It was like that with the 100 Club. Downstairs, with its low ceiling, poor acoustics and 250 sweating people, it was like a giant garage. It had no fire regulations but a great atmosphere.

Our lyrics represented the rawness of the terraces and the BBC took an interest in us, as only the BBC can, following us around for a *40 Minutes* programme. You talk honestly on camera, thinking that you're gonna get a fair crack of the whip, until someone gets it into the cutting room – then you're just ratings fodder. 'You should have known that,' everyone said. Easy to say with the benefit of hindsight.

Record deals are what it's all about, but when a SK advance looked like being in the offing an anonymous journalist (rumoured to be Gary Bushell of the *NME*) wrote that we were extremist and neo-Nazis. That, combined with the BBC's *40 Minutes*, which showed fights breaking out at our Harlow concert, ended our musical aspirations. Our final fling was a trip to the Brixton Academy, where Attilla the Stockbroker was playing, to have a quiet word with Gary Bushell. Gary wasn't there so Attilla copped it instead. We went on stage and smashed his ukulele over his head. Without a recording contract there was no point in continuing the band, and the fact was that another trend was taking over.

The death of white power music occurred one terrifying night in the Hambro Tavern in Southall, when a huge crowd of 1,000

Pakistanis and Indians marched on the pub and burned it to the ground. For a few hairy hours, the police had their backs to the wall while west London exploded. Jimmy and Peter Clark, who normally followed The Satellites, were there. Caught the night train to another country, bussing in the white people to play, but racial segregation doesn't exist in London or any other part of England, does it? That's what they tell us. Admittedly it was provocative, because everybody knew that Southall wasn't really England but might as well have been part of India. There were 'white noise' bands that The Satellites had a big west London following, but west London ended abruptly where Hayes met Southall. Driving through Hayes, you come to the Western International Market, then across the canal bridge and . . . welcome to Calcutta. That night, the Paki inhabitants of Southall scotched the myth that they were all shopkeepers, torching everything with waves of petrol bombs. Rumour has it that the police and white lads stood shoulder to shoulder while the flames licked at them. After that, no promoter would touch The Four Skins or any other skinhead band.

Music was the food of love in the mid-'80s, and the catalyst for the end of the mobs attacking each other. In a series of field meetings, Leeds, Millwall and Chelsea met in a pub in Victoria and talked about E distribution at the main rave parties in the mid-'80s, the confrontation went out of football and the lads started to love each other as they dropped pills by the fistful. Bombed out on Es, the idea of fighting somebody on a Saturday afternoon became a tiresome afterthought to the eight hours of dancing to exhaustion which were to follow. Sitting around cross-legged and tripping, the aggression evaporated. Also they were earning loads of money. Getting nicked or chased along some grotty street by a dozen half-wits trying to slash your face, or earning a monkey selling pills to those you had once terrorised? It was no contest.

STRIctly caSUAL

'STANNUM! EVENING STANNUM!' shouted the paper seller. *'Evening Standard! Evening Standard!'* was what he was actually shouting, but somehow it always sounded like 'Stannum'. Hotdogs, hamburgers, programmes: all the vendors outside Chelsea vied for the money of the punters heading into the ground. Now, in the late '70s, a new sound joined their cries: *'Bulldog, Bulldog,* get your copy of the young National Front's paper.' Plenty of Chelsea fans purchased the paper – not because they were interested in politics, but for the league table of louts on the back page. Chelsea, Leeds and West Ham were regularly in the top three. Fans would purchase it just to be able to tell their mates they'd read it first. A small hard-core stood outside with shaven heads and a belief in what we were doing, despite the fact that at the time the best-known face at Chelsea, Babs, was black. He had been featured in *The Sun* as a Chelsea leader. One day a West Ham fan mocked us with this fact. 'You're full of shit, you lot. Look at who your top boy is.' We must have looked pissed off at that, because it made them look even more smug than they usually do. We knew what he meant. Babs was the Chelsea top boy in a world where white was right. Football aggro had once been the preserve of white working-class boys and now the blacks were seen as muscling in. Just like all the dance floors in London had been occupied only by white boys shuffling around to black

James Brown feel-good songs, the young blacks were now coming to the fore in football.

'Babs has black skin but he ain't a nigger.' Nobody ever saw Babs as anything other than Chelsea. It was the same everywhere in England. All that racist crap and 'nigger' shit is for places like America. For instance, the time Muhammed Ali fought Sonny Liston in the deep south of America, a strung-out redneck shouted: 'Sonny Liston. Knock that nigger out.' Why bother explaining the vagaries of niggers and black skin to someone as dumb as that? In years to come, those white-only fans would embrace plenty of dark-skinned lads into their firms as top boys, but for now they stuck their chests out and said they were staying true to the Enoch Powell ethos. The closer to the action you got, the more you needed people who had bottle. Blacks showed plenty of bottle when it came to it. Skin colour never came into it.

Along with the twins from Arsenal, Babs and Black Jim were one of the main movers and shakers in London United, a skinhead thing which started in 1975. It was around for five or six years, and revolved around groups going up to the Cockney Pride pub for some serious northerner-bashing on a Friday night. Northerners coming down to London on a Friday for a night out soon realised that their problems didn't just start on a Saturday when they met 200 London skins. We'd all seen the film *Warriors* and now some of us were living it for real.

Everybody used to meet in the Crown and Shuttle, just past Liverpool Street station. The alliance was doomed to failure after Babs and Steve Woods from West Ham had a straightener there. West Ham immediately turned the fight into a football thing – after all, Liverpool Street was their manor. That was where all the Essex boys caught the train home after a day working in the city. West Ham let it be known that Chelsea fans had better not show. Without us, it was bound to lack serious numbers.

There were those who stated, with some conviction, that they hated blacks, but they never checked the colour of their skin was when it looked like it was going to come on top. In a tear-up, everyone was the same colour. The myth that blacks had no bottle was dispelled time and time again as Chelsea travelled.

At a National Front march along the Walworth Road during the 1978–79 football season, the usual array of left-wing protestors were lined up. At the Elephant and Castle, two black faces, Steff from Chelsea and Denton from Arsenal, were recognised by the Chelsea lads on the march, and came over.

'Hello lads, how's it going?' Denton asked.

'What the fuck are you doing here?' asked Bulldog from Arsenal.

The other people in the march looked dumbfounded at these two blacks appearing, but this was football and there was the firm's honour at stake: 'It's a skins thing. Skins against the rest. Who needs these Anti-Nazi League poofs trying to be good white boys protecting us poor black chaps? I don't want some bunch of northerners and scruffy militant lefties fighting for me against Chelsea boys. That's for us to see to on the terraces,' was the way Denton put it. 'Skinheads together fight the Reds, eh Denton,' added one of the other Chelsea lads, referring slyly to the fact that Denton was an Arsenal fan.

In fact, many of the early Chelsea characters, not just Babs, were black. Walking up the steps into the Shed end from the main entrance, you'd immediately meet Kojak. Tall and dark with all-knowing eyes, he stood and watched everyone like he was counting the fans in, making sure that those who should be in attendance were there, nodding to those he needed to show respect to. There were no interlopers in his end. Getting a nod off Kojak was an acknowledgement that you'd made the grade in the recognition stakes. His time-warp-stuck uniform of flares and stacked heels stayed with him for years. He also wore a denim waistcoat which he'd had cut down to show off a little more muscle. The police gave him a kind of respect, because when they told him to move on, as they did frequently, he would give them his best frown as if to say: 'Officer, go and catch real criminals.' Some young hothead PC trying to make a name would say, 'Move it or I'll eject you, sooty.' Kojak always responded gently:

'Don't touch the threads, man,' he would say, pushing the officer's arm away from his waistcoat and ignoring the sambo or sooty jibes. He got thrown out plenty of times, but he never called no policeman 'bwana'.

Then there was Black Jim, who always went on about the '70s. 'What's 'appening?' he'd say, giving you a low five. High fives were still the preserve of the Harlem Globetrotters and were seen as uncool by London blacks. It was unnecessary to reply, for Jim always knew what was happening. He was the first person to wear Converse baseball boots at football matches, in the days when only one shop in England, based on the King's Road, imported them. Jim predicted the trainer revolution in the days when only a pair of DMs afforded credibility. When everyone started wearing Adidas Gazelles in loads of different colours, Jim stated knowingly that he'd dumped better in the bin and Converse cream was the only colour to be seen in.

'Nothing much happening there, Jim,' you'd reply.

'No way, man, something must be happening. There's always something going down, if you know what I mean,' he'd reply.

Then you'd smile and walk away, because even if you didn't know what the hell he was talking about it sounded good, plus Jim knew all about Converse before the marketing man at Nike had finished his college degree.

Jim was the type of black person who looked like he was dancing when he was standing still and could look like he was really moving when he was only jigging slightly to the rhythm of a song, standing on the edge of a dance floor. 'Come on, baby, do the tighten up,' he'd sing, or he'd screech the intro to his favourite Archie Bell and the Drells song, 'Here I Go Again': 'Here I go, here I go, here I go.' Looking at Jim, we knew we had no rhythm. That was his greatest compliment to us whiteys – a Chelsea boy with rhythm. 'I can tell by the way you move you got soul,' he'd say.

The terraces became the early show-out areas for the blacks before they took over the discos. The media said that blacks were intimidated by the racial abuse at Chelsea, but I couldn't see that

– nobody saw that except them. Jim wasn't black, he was Chelsea in Converse. Leeds were far more racist than Chelsea. Sure, there was a group of racists at Chelsea who hated it when Paul Cannonville became the first black player to wear the blue shirt, but nobody called it racist when Spurs fans, who were predominantly Jewish, gave some of their players abuse because they didn't like them. Dave Hill, the journalist, pointed out that white boys only abuse black football players at games because they haven't got the courage to do it in the streets, but that was his fear talking, not ours. We abused because we were the crowd. Abuse is good. If the working man couldn't scream at players and other teams on a Saturday afternoon, he'd stay at home with his TV control and WWF wrestling. Even now, the press tells us that Indians don't attend football because of fear. More likely they're too busy taking an extra £2 in the till at the corner shop.

'Stab him. Stab him,' the voice shouted in the Shed every time the opposition did anything to a Chelsea player. In fact, this was shouted every time something happened. For instance, the police would charge in and grab a fan. As he was being dragged out, the shout would go up: 'Stab him!' A police officer got really annoyed one time and moved through the crowd to get the fan who later became known as Ima Lemmon to everyone. Eventually this lone police officer grabbed a fan and dragged him out proclaiming that he'd got 'Stab man', until he got a few paces down and the cry 'Stab him too' went up. Then the ironic cheers rang out, the philharmonic accompaniment. Alongside 'Zigger', it was the best-known Shed chant. Hickey came along with his North Stand Song, the Ramones derivative 'Hit Him On The Head': 'Hit him on the head with a baseball bat, oh yeah.' The Manchester City boys took it up as their own and it echoed vibrantly across the Kippax, the giant terrace that ran the length of their pitch.

Card-carrying BNP members stood next to the new generation of black fans at Chelsea and chanted their monkey noises at opposing black players, or shouted out 'black bastard' to opposing coloured players. 'Nothing personal mate,' they'd say. No offence was taken. They would all go outside and stand side by side in a toe-to-toe with the opposing fans. The guys who did boo Paul Cannonville got more credence than their actions deserved.

Martin Webster, chairman of the National Front, looked at the thousands of young white men confronting each other every other Saturday and recognised an energy that he wanted to harness. Joe Pearce, the young NF organiser, bemoaned the fact that while Chelsea could muster 35,000 fanatical fans every other Saturday and 2,000 nutters when they were away to charge out of the railway station, the NF couldn't summon 200 lads on a warm, sunny summer afternoon in London for a NF march even when there was no football on. The NF never managed to solve that conundrum.

It was easy, really; the NF didn't carry any clout and politics is boring. Football wasn't just sport – it was a part of us, bred into our psyche, the reason we got up every day. Standing alongside your mates at Chelsea was about the respect of your team, and self-respect, like the 'pride of the regiment' stuff that made Maggie Thatcher boast that British troops were the finest in the world. We stood for the values, in a misguided way. But politics had no focal point, no real characters or history, at least not for English people. Politicians were old gits who'd never done anything remotely exciting. They wanted to control with words not deeds so how could we empathise with them? Although the average white lad fighting at football might have stated that he hated blacks, he didn't really – mostly we didn't care. We'd chant 'blacks out' during the day, then dance to the Motown sound of the Elgin's 'Heaven Must Have Sent You' in the evening.

A small group stood outside the Shed selling *Bulldog*. Joe Pearce, whose brother was in Soft Cell, read more into it than there really was. As if young white English people were ever going to immerse themselves in politics. They'd moan about having to sing 'Ba Ba Green Sheep' or shake their heads at the banning of golliwog badges, but football was never about racism, even if the Anti-Nazi League chose to see it that way.

'Free Robert Relf. Free Robert Relf,' chanted football terraces around England. This was in the 'glorious' '70s when the white Englishman tried to choose what colour of person he would sell his house to. It was a short-lived shout which echoed around the terraces. Relf, a dipstick from the Midlands, put a sign up saying he wouldn't sell his house to a black man and as a reward the Ministry jailed him. The popular press started one of their campaigns which died quickly.

The NF boys put out rumours of a confrontation. The word got out that the Anti-Nazi League were going to protest outside the Shed because more copies of *Bulldog* were sold in Chelsea than anywhere else in England. What sort of firm would they be mustering? They'd need plenty if they were going to make a show. The Chelsea boys would have treated them the same as any other firm who tried to take liberties at Chelsea, would even have told them that they hated their politics, might even have stated that they hated blacks to give an extra edge to the confrontation, but the Anti-Nazi League didn't show. Smart move, boys.

The National Front and the BNP were never about colour, but were more about what you represented and the belonging thing. There were those who were fanatics, but they exist in all walks of life. The irony of it was that sometimes the *Socialist Worker* was on sale right next to us. They gave up in the end, because nobody bought it outside the ground. If they'd put a hooligan league table on the back, it would have been a different matter.

The NF were anti-black, whereas we were just pro-football. Belonging to a football firm gave us everything we needed: comradeship, mates and the chance of excitement and travel. The NF only offered us the chance to march along the road, chanting their slogans, and transferring our power to their leaders.

'What do we want? Enoch Powell. When do we want him? Now.' What did that mean? Nothing. Nobody took it seriously. Football fans adored their team and its players, not some silly twit in a pinstripe suit with an Oxbridge accent.

Chelsea scoring was fun, but this wasn't. Enoch Powell was a loser, the man who had made the 'Rivers of Blood' speech and was sacked for his trouble. Also he was an intellectual, and, like most intellectuals, would have looked down his nose at us. I can just imagine Martin Webster sitting here, reading his *Sun* newspaper, while Enoch studied one of the classics; in the original Greek, of course. The man spoke seven languages. He wouldn't have been able to comprehend us, any more than we could him.

On Saturday, standing shoulder-to-shoulder with thousands of others, singing, was something we dreamed about all week.

'You're going to get your fucking heads kicked in. You're going home in a fucking ambulance.'

Elgar, Bernstein, Lennon and McCartney. You write a classic tune and we'll put a football lyric to it.

For a while, the British Movement, which was fiercely anti-semitic and anti-communist, offered comradeship with paramilitary training, but the boys saw something faggoty in all the 'leader guard protecting the upper hierarchy' rubbish. When someone found out that it was modelled on the Hitler guard, they were appalled. 'Pretending to be German – you're joking! We hate Germans.'

The fashion of the late '70s couldn't last, that was for sure. Even those who were diehards are now embarrassed by the pictures. Checked Oxford bags, 32-inch flares. Thank God England never qualified for any World Cup tournaments in '74 and '78 and the boys never travelled away. They couldn't put the boot in properly because of the wind factor. Scarves were tied around the wrist. What did those Manchester boys look like with their checked scarves and Bay City Rollers' fashion influence? Teenage rampage? They had to be joking. The glorious pictures from the seventies when Man U invaded the pitch and put the boot in with six-inch wedge heels.

The casual scene came along around 1981–82. It coincided with a split in Combat 84, and everybody embraced it wholeheartedly. After punk came the New Romantics. For a while the Gooners had a small New Romantic group, but the young Arsenal firm, the Herd, really loved the whole casual thing. While Spandau Ballet gave it the big chant, 'Don't Need This Pressure', all the main faces were doing the Stray Cat Strut. Being hard wasn't just about the company you kept or even your numbers but was also about the way you looked when you did the business.

Pringle and Lyle & Scott jumpers abounded at Chelsea. Some days it was like a youth golf convention, there were so many on display. The fashion stakes went up: Gabbicci tops, Farah slacks and Lois jumbo cords. Levi jeans were in, but woe betide anybody who wore a pair without the right width at the ankle line. The merest hint of a flare was a recipe for ridicule, except for Hickey that is, who wore flying goggles, ridiculous full-length trench coat, and brown 32-hole lace-up DM boots. Everyone laughed at Hickey and he laughed back. 'You're so into fashion you're all bloody victims and prisoners,' was his retort. 'Look at you lot, sheep, every one. Those label owners must see the pound signs every time you walk over the threshold.'

It didn't deter us and the fashion parade went on. Brown Apollo boots, the famed desert boots, were the preferred footwear after trainers. They looked good on a Chelsea mob marching along, but a Birmingham crowd wearing them looked like pathetic dumb asses. One day they got the full works. First Giles looked them up and down: 'Poor colour and label co-ordination,' he proclaimed loudly.

'What do they look like? A bunch of primary school children, they'll be wearing Clark's sandals next,' shouted Hickey at a giant group of Birmingham boys outside New Street station. 'Great for running in, though, lads.' They were completely useless for kicking somebody, more likely to break your foot than to do any damage. Worse than that, those who weren't in the know would buy the Freeman Hardy Willis imitation desert boot, usually some stupid northern crew. Now the insults changed from 'You lot are all cowards' to 'You lot are so sad, you wear FHW desert boots'.

One day the Arsenal mob, black and white together dressed

head to toe in their best designer threads, stood by the fence in the North Stand and started shouting that the Chelsea élite, by now inhabiting Gate 13, were wearing flared trousers and were fashion losers. Holding their trousers above the ankle, they yelled: 'Don't flare up, boys, you'll discover fashion one day.' This was the ultimate insult to us. The Adidas Trim-Tram trainers were cool. Adidas Gazelles were passable, until the scousers started wearing them. Seeing hundreds of pairs of red Gazelles retreating up the King's Road after an ambush on a Saturday would have been an adman's wet dream. Not that the scousers were bothered. While the Chelsea lads were paying them out, they were using the diversion to demolish the windows of the jewellers' shops in the Edgware Road.

One Saturday, Giles came in with a pair of Borg Elite trainers. This wasn't just posing, it was elevating the word into the stratosphere. Each pair had a card which showed what number of person you were in the purchase order. For a few Saturdays after that, it became *de rigueur* for everyone to compare cards. It put a whole new slant on the phrase 'card-carrying hooligans'. Some of the guys even started drinking tomato juice with a dash of Worcester sauce: 'It looks good, doesn't it?' 'You lot would drink camel shit and bus tickets as long as it looked good,' was Hickey's mocking response. Then the press informed us that the new designer hooligans had eschewed alcohol in order to keep a clearer mind for fighting. That certainly wasn't true at Chelsea, although spilling beer on the designer label threads was not good for the image.

In the pub before matches, people compared Lacoste jumpers and polos and looked to see who was wearing what. Heads were turned, not by pretty girls, but by someone wearing something different. Pre-match talk was now about Galiano, John Paul Gaultier and the cut of a Paul Smith suit. The ultimate insult was someone feeling the quality of your threads and declaring them to be real Aquascutum, in a mocking voice. The older guys, who we nicknamed the puncher brigade, were appalled by our attitude.

Then came the Tachini track-suits. One afternoon Chelsea

ambushed Spurs at Parson's Green. It was the usual disjointed charge of the belligerents grunting and puffing. At 30 paces the Spurs lads turned into a rag-tag army and bolted across the park. Impromptu scuffles broke out when a few turned and stood. As the pandemonium spread it looked comically chaotic, with people shouting, punching and kicking. One of the older guys remarked that it looked like Bjorn Borg's army doing battle with John McEnroe's. He stood in the middle of the designer mayhem shaking his head, unable to decide who to punch. He grabbed someone. 'Who the fuck are you?' he asked aggressively, holding the poor guy by his throat.

'Chelsea,' the guy gurgled back.

'Chelsea? Why don't you dress like Chelsea, then?' He shook his head. 'This is bollocks,' he shouted. 'Oh, for the simple days of scarves, Harrington jackets, bleached Levis and DMs, when we knew what we were fighting against. I can't keep up with all this fashion crap,' he sighed, then cleared off back to his pint in the White Hart.

Designer days out meant that sometimes you'd be somewhere and would suddenly be in the midst of a rival mob before you knew what had happened. This was especially true in London derbies where, apart from the main faces, it was usually designer chaos with even the police getting confused about who was who. Many times people were caught and had to decide to run or walk along with their mouths shut, eyes front, taking a deep breath, and hoping that they might be ignored. The worst feeling was being caught up with the opposition and surrounded by loads of Old Bill and just when you thought you'd got away with it and were about to slip away, you would suddenly hear the sound of phlegm coming up and a big green wad would be deposited on your back. That was usually repeated four or five times – there was nothing you could do about it. Before slipping away the guy who had clocked you would say, 'See you around, green back.'

There were days when it seemed that wherever you went Chelsea was waiting to punch and kick individuals who were too cocky for their own good. Right into 'em they went. Plenty were waiting for it because everyone knew that they couldn't leave – they were addicted to the fight.

Saturday shoppers heading home after a day in Oxford Street were startled by the outbreak of a fight. Top Shop, Woodhouse and Swank plastic carrier bags fell to the floor as people scattered. Women held their children as people leaped the barriers to get one good punch in before the police, charging out of the back of a waiting van, got it under control. It was over in seconds, with individuals being led away, protesting their innocence.

——————

There's still a feeling of nostalgia for the days of lads and beer, when women didn't go to football. There was no reason for it really, no misogyny, they just didn't go, it was purely a lads' thing. Now we have the heart-on-the-sleeve Nick Hornby generation showing the world their feminine side, more women have started attending. I'm not sure about that, but in the old days, any girl going to a football match was fair game to be chatted up and pulled by the boys who fancied themselves. Some of them were serial pullers and never went anywhere without coming home with a telephone number, but despite their boasting in the pub the following week, it was usually the exception rather than the rule. The funniest characters were the serial monsters, who couldn't pull in any club south of Rejkjavick but suddenly thought they'd become Richard Gere just because they were north of Watford and had a cockney accent.

'Hello, girls, I'm from London.'

'Really, I thought you'd escaped from a very dark cellar,' was the funniest reply I ever heard, uttered by a very startled but sharp girl with a broad South Yorkshire accent in Sheffield one afternoon, when accosted by one of our uglier travelling brethren. That was all the pretty boys needed to deter them from putting an arm around her. Don't worry, darling, I'll protect you from these London oafs.

Liz Cubitt, or Chelsea Liz to her friends, came to a few away matches. On the infamous opening-day battle of Brighton in 1983–84, she got arrested for kicking a copper outside a bar. The policeman had been roughing her up, so she planted a beauty of a size six across his shins and got fined £100 for her trouble. The only thing was that she had booked the B&B and it was only when she didn't turn up in the pub later that the lads knew they had a problem. 'Never trust a woman to do anything,' was Mark Cator's response. They spent a cold evening dressed in their best summer civvies, shivering on the platform at Brighton railway station. The smart ones caught the train into Gatwick and sat in the warmth of the airport before travelling back to Victoria the next day.

Other girls did go sometimes. Eddie Durkin was often seen with two girls from Hackney. The more cynical amongst us used to attribute this to the fact that being with two girls meant he could shy away from violence. Nobody, not even the lowest of the low, would hit a girl fan. It was okay to shower them with abuse, but not to use physical violence against them.

———

Wherever you went, there was always a pub meeting place. It was usually unplanned and the spontaneity of the crowd made it impossible for the police to keep any control of our movements. Inevitably, people spilled out onto the forecourt or pavement and always without fail the opposing mob would turn up for a recce, only to be put to flight by an Agincourt-level barrage of glasses and bottles.

The noise of hundreds of breakable flying objects smashing together created a crescendo of sound, the horn section of our orchestra. Seconds after the solo the accompaniment of sirens can be heard, then the screech of tyres as police vans fly in and officers jump out holding their helmets, slamming doors, unsure of what is happening, running around doing the headless chicken pushing people and shouting. 'Get back inside the pub, you lot,' yells an exasperated police superintendent. But it was as if he'd walked onto a beach moments after a giant wave had swept across the sand, leaving calm but also a trail of devastation in its wake. Then it was back to the pints while a few waited for a re-run.

Of course, it never really happened like that.

One Saturday some of the older guys ambushed a group of Tottenham fans going to Fulham for a match, after catching them slipping in early in the morning: some of the boys loved those early-morning ambushes. One of them had purchased some Domestos and took great pleasure in tipping it over a prostrate Spurs fan, telling him he'd just destroyed his credibility: 'Bleached tracksuits, whatever next?'

Hickey and a few of the older boys came back into the pub laughing their heads off at the bleach on the tracksuits and also an incident with a police dog. As the lads chased the Spurs fans along the Fulham Palace Road, a policeman jumped out with a dog, then let it go. As it ran towards the Chelsea mob, someone squirted ammonia in its face and the dog went wild, biting everything in sight, including its handler. The police officer went berserk and wanted to murder every Chelsea fan, screaming: 'I'm gonna kill you all.' Someone pulled out a carving knife and it ended up in the mad policeman's shoulder. Hickey and a few of the others got back on the tube. Just before the doors shut, three policemen jumped on, all sweaty and panting, as if they'd been running along the road.

One of the policemen turned to his mate.

'Did you see what happened to Jeff's dog?'

'Yes, wasn't it terrible?'

'And what about Jeff? Did you see what happened to Jeff?'

'Oh, yes, that was terrible too.'

Only in England could a bunch of policemen consider a dog's fate before that of their colleague. The lads held their laughter until they got off at Fulham Broadway.

Spurs never bothered us. It was a long walk from the Seven

Sisters tube to the ground and there were plenty of pubs along the route, filled with Spurs boys who only pretended they wanted to know. Mind you, the boys in the Bull pub used to stand outside really giving it plenty. Then there was the Corner Pin mob, all mouth and trousers, safe in the knowledge that there were more police per square foot than there were of us, and within 20 paces, so that nobody would start anything. Who wants to get that close to the ground only to get nicked for knocking out a Sly Stallone lookalike? The Tottenham lot would stand in their typical pose, short-sleeved T-shirt, pint in the left hand, right fist conveniently positioned behind the bicep to pump up the muscle a little bit.

New meeting points became necessary as the police grew better at exchanging information, so the lads had reinstated the old '70s meeting points which had fooled the police for a short while. Waterloo used to be a great place to meet, but it had the worst pub ever. It was called The Drum, and it looked like someone had built a spiral staircase then decided to slap some glass on the outside and make it into a pub. Upstairs was a bar and there were usually a gaggle of world-weary commuters straight off the Waterloo & City line having a quick pint before heading back to suburbia. You got the impression that the pint they were drinking was the only way they could brave the monotony of the train once more. In the late summer months you'd catch the smell of sweat and wool, the result of too many bodies packed together on the underground. Our youthful expectation and shiny-bright designer colours contrasted vividly with their dark, creased suits and air of dissatisfaction.

Football fans would meet for a drink in The Drum before Saturday matches. Always behind the bar there was a disinterested employee serving pints. Order ten and they would always forget how many they had poured, meaning you'd only have to pay for eight. They also had automatic dispensers, so everybody argued that the amount served was less than a pint and more chaos ensued.

There is no better feeling than walking towards somewhere with no police escort, knowing that you've got the boys on board to give it to them. Once we put the windows of the Bull in, no Spurs fans came out. Suddenly the landlord appeared with two giant Rottweilers. They were snarling and barking, but only for a few seconds until the CS gas hit them square in the face. Back into the pub they ran yelping and crying, but not before biting the landlord, who stood there open-mouthed in shock, until a friendly right-hander caught him side on, causing him to stagger backwards on baby giraffe legs, then he too went back inside at speed. At the ground, 200 forged tickets for one seat meant more chaos – our best friend. If the police could impose order they were happy but as soon as they lost it, the advantage switched to our modus operandi.

———

Even though we never had any trouble from them, there is something about Spurs which makes everybody want to beat them. They were always harking on about the past, the Glory, Glory days. Danny Blanchflower was once a great player for Spurs but the worst manager Chelsea ever had. One year, Glasgow Rangers came down in August for a pre-season friendly with Tottenham. The Rangers fans spent the day drinking to excess in the West End around Trafalgar Square, before travelling to the Spurs ground on buses. By the time the buses hit the Tottenham High Road the Rangers fans were hanging out the back of buses, throwing bottles at any blacks who passed, pissing out of the emergency exits and causing complete mayhem. The ferocity of their attacks on the Asian shopkeepers who trade all along the Seven Sisters road shocked the police and locals alike.

A small crowd of Chelsea had gone along with some Rangers fans we had got friendly with. As we approached the ground, a bus came past and screeched to a halt. The bus driver, looking extremely harassed, jumped out in disgust, shouting 'Animals!' Three Rangers fans clutching whisky bottles alighted and were jumped on by a number of police, who told them they were being arrested. A mêlée developed with one drunken Rangers fan falling down and taking the policemen who were holding him with him. As they rolled about on the ground, people walking past laughed at the spectacle. One of the policemen recognised us and said: 'Give us your lot any day. This lot are mad.'

Whilst the average British person has more interest in origami than religion, the same cannot be said for the Glaswegian supporters of Rangers and Celtic. Up there it is war, with both teams' colours reflecting their religious affiliations. There were a number of people at Chelsea who were staunch Rangers fans. It was through them that I became interested in Scottish football and attended a few games. Having attended many matches, I have to say that there is nothing quite like a Glasgow derby.

Kenny Salford was so pro-Rangers that he wouldn't have anything green in his house. Rumour had it that he once asked if it was possible to buy blue grass seed. When told it wasn't, he concreted over his lawn. Salford was forever talking about William of Orange and the Battle of the Boyne. He organised mini-bus trips up to matches and when Chelsea played Rangers in a pre-season friendly in the early '80s, a lot of friendships were made. The Glasgow Rangers mob were also called the ICF – the Inter Crown Firm, such was their allegiance to the crown. When they sang at football it wasn't just about the team, it meant so much more. No Chelsea fan who ever went up there for a Glasgow derby could fail to feel a tingle of excitement when 50,000 people started singing with a religious fervour. Glasgow as a city has a fearsome reputation for violence, but by 1990 it had acquired the status of City of Culture. It was certainly buzzing every time we went up there.

Scots are not supposed to like the English, but that is unfounded, because they are much more open and friendly than Londoners generally, who tend to keep you at arm's length. One thing for sure, though, jocks are drink monsters, especially at football. If there's anything alcoholic at a football match they'll consume it, in huge quantities. Rangers fans are also the original football nutters. Once during an infamous riot in Spain, the police let their dogs go and it is rumoured that the Rangers fans bit the dogs then threw them back. The dogs never went back for seconds.

There were always 12 to 14 people on the bus to Glasgow. Some, like Salford, were into the Protestant thing, while others were just guys out for a good laugh. It did cause problems though, especially when we started meeting in the North London Tavern in Kilburn, which had a large percentage of IRA sympathisers.

Salford had arranged a Glasgow pub meet at 10.30 a.m. We were together in an Orange Lodge pub. Personally, I understand what that means, but to the average Chelsea fan Orange means Holland. Normally when you meet the lads for a match at Chelsea and you say 10.30 a.m., the pub is empty and people are still drifting in at around 1 p.m. Here, the place was heaving when we arrived, alive with noise and singing. One of the younger Chelsea lads nearly caused a riot when he asked the barman: 'Why do all the royal family pictures have orange sashes painted on them?'

One of the stewards came over looking very stern faced, unable to believe his question was serious: 'Sort your boys out. Asking questions like that.' He walked away shaking his head.

Another time we went to a Rangers v Celtic match and one of the Chelsea lads had on a pale green Lyle & Scott sweater. The doorman at the bar refused him entry until he removed it.

One weekend Rangers were playing Aberdeen on the Saturday, and Chelsea were playing in Manchester on the Sunday. Aberdeen had a little mob called the Casuals. Their main face, Jay Allen, has written a book about his exploits as a football hooligan. Matches like this were not much fun usually because no one was much interested in Scottish football, it was more about having a giggle and going to something different. Some Chelsea fans showed a real interest in Scottish football though, and one day at the Skol Cup final I also saw two well-known Spurs fans, Sunny and Winston, following Rangers.

It is much colder in Scotland than it is in London. The Aberdeen lads called themselves casuals although we couldn't imagine their image of casuals could ever have been that casual, because they would certainly have had to have worn coats. Everybody knew that casual meant shirt label on display. Over the horizon Adidas and Tommy Hilfiger would proclaim their names from the back of jackets but that was a fashion statement from beyond the grave unless you counted those dorks who wore donkey jackets to winter midweek matches with Wimpy Construction emblazoned across the shoulder blades. Contempt beyond explanation. It was cold, but the Linfield fan who was with us was not acknowledging it. His trip to Rangers was partly a religious pilgrimage. His Northern Ireland loyalism was crossing the Irish sea, and would be displayed at the match for all those Fenian Celtic bastards to see. So he sat there with his Linfield shirt on. Just above his heart, on the other side of his chest, was a rosette with a picture of Prince Charles and Lady Diana in the middle. It didn't matter how cold he felt, he would make his religious statement. You have to admire the crass stubbornness of people like that, even if they are completely bonkers.

One weekend we arrived in Glasgow and the inclement Scots weather saw the cancellation of the Rangers match. Celtic were playing Hearts, and 14 of us went in. We entered the ground through Gate 12, which led into the notorious terrace called the Jungle. Halfway through the first half, we unfurled a Union Jack flag with Chelsea written in the middle. The response was amazing. The only word to describe it is 'mental'. A terrace surge like ones which were common in the '70s came at us. It was a human wave of pure anger. People were spitting and snarling. Luckily for us, the police removed us and our flag then ejected us from the ground, taking us back to our coach and telling us to leave Glasgow. 'As if we haven't got enough problems up here without some stupid Chelsea fans unfurling a Union Jack flag inside a Celtic game.'

In one bar in Glasgow, Daddy Warbucks, one of the Chelsea lads, played the machine and at the end put his initials as one of the top scores. He signed it CFC UVF, which meant that every time the Celtic fans walked past the machine they would see those words. It was like a red rag to a bull and Daddy Warbucks hoped that his little flourish would cause all the Celtic fans in the pub to play the machine all night to get those initials off it. As soon as the first one saw those hated words, though, the mood turned very nasty. Within minutes there would have been a Braveheart-type charge, so Giles jumped behind the counter, pushed the barmaid out of the way, saying, 'Trust me, darling, I'm a retailer,' pressed the no-sale button, and then whipped out the whole till tray and gassed the bar, while we scarpered.

A couple of Rangers fans once told one of the travelling Chelsea lads that most Rangers supporters didn't go to Scotland matches. He couldn't get his head round that. 'What, do you mean you don't support your own country?' he asked incredulously, then shook his head and walked away.

Manchester might have dominated the music and club scene during the 1980s, but it still seemed unwelcoming, for it always rained in bucket loads whenever Chelsea went up there. Rain and casual-wear don't mix. One Saturday it was overcast in London and absolutely pissing down in Manchester. At that time brown brushed-suede jackets were fashionable. After ten minutes in the rain, those things weigh a hundredweight. After four hours they weigh in at just under a ton. That Saturday, our suede jackets absorbed so much water that everybody thought their arms had stretched a few inches.

The casual look was not practical. It was designed to look good, not to keep you warm. Non-functionals was how Hickey described us. 'What do you lot look like in this English Baltic climate?' he liked to say, when he saw the shivering collective. While the punchers brigade dressed in their winter jackets, we looked on in disgust. Overcoats, sheepskin jackets. Are you sure boys? How could you not want to out-fashion your opposite number? To the old 'uns, being seen shivering at an away game was an indication of cowardice, but the casual look demanded that designer labels were always fully on show. Despite football being a winter game, it didn't stop the boys going to matches dressed to kill. Sometimes it got so cold that people turned as blue as Chelsea's shirts.

Oldham must be one of the coldest grounds in England. The wind seems to blow direct from Siberia, turn left at the Pennines and whistle across the away end. Oldham is close to Manchester and had a firm called the Fine Young Casuals. They were voted as hardy fools for wearing casual gear in such a cold climate, but they never had enough numbers to bother Chelsea so the boys were always looking for an after-match skirmish with the Manchester United Red Army or the Manchester City chaps. Manchester boys dressed the part as well. If we'd humiliated them but didn't out-fashion them it wouldn't have been a true off, so the boys went dressed to thrill and kill.

One day at Oldham it was so cold that the lads were asking the police to throw them out to get some warmth back into their bones. You could see the glee in the policemen's faces when they realised that they would get to lock everybody in for at least 40 minutes after the match. It was too cold to even want to look for trouble – some of the lads' joints were frozen up – let alone try to run people. On returning to London, one fan thought about writing to the FA to try and get football declared a summer sport.

———

Going away was all about mainline stations and new conversations. On these occasions everybody was a Kojak in his own right, nodding and getting nods in return. There were never enough seats on the concourse, so everyone waiting for a train was forced to stand around, making those who frequented the station for everyday mundane purposes wary of our motives. We couldn't stand still, had to be up and moving as the frenetic energy of expectation made us twitchy. We looked as though we were loitering with intent but in reality we were just waiting for a train. The police were unable to move us on because the reason for waiting was right there. All they could do was make noise and hassle with 'move on, don't bunch here' expressions of their exasperation.

Fans from different clubs mingled in and around the numerous cafés serving over-priced sandwiches with soggy edges where the fillings had been absorbed by the bread, wrinkly cellophane-wrapped pies and pasties – brown, hard pastry with congealed fat and gristle attached to the meat.

'This food's shit,' was a frequent complaint. 'So why buy it then, you goon?' And the stories unfolded by the minute over mugs of stewed British Rail tea. Someone made a classic comment over breakfast one morning: 'Gentlemen, there are 3,000 scousers out there. Our mission is to find a few of them and batter them senseless.' People talked of missions and success rates, good days and bad days. They read the tabloid newspapers but could have been quoting from any one of thousands of management theory books, yet they'd never read one in their life. Spooky.

On a trip back from Manchester when the Stretford End was eclipsed, Hickey made his famous announcement (although all his announcements were famous): 'This is the Day of Infamy. Drink it in, boys, because it doesn't come any better than this.'

In ten minutes outside King's Cross on a Saturday morning, everybody knew who'd been run and where. Estimates of how many were due in – sometimes Christmas came early. With no police around, a small group of scousers might think that an 8 a.m. arrival was in the comfort zone. A few impromptu smacks in the teeth would soon put paid to that theory. Seeing them leap the barriers and scoot off into the King's Cross back streets was a regular sight, witnessed by the sad, stinking-clothed winos who littered the pavements with their sweet sherry bottles. It was funny how the scousers were always up with the lark, more so than any other firm.

In those days, before closed-circuit TV and hand-held video cameras, the police watched everybody intently, checking tickets at the barriers, the British Rail employees with their scruffy, dirty uniforms trying to maintain an air of authority by constricting the space at the ticket gate. 'Change your shirt, you dirty git, there's enough grease on that collar to fry chips.'

It was a different class in those days, we made the police work for their money. They tried to second-guess what we were up to and what would unfold. Didn't you just love it when the Sunday papers would print hundreds of pictures of poor Plod running around absolutely clueless about what was happening.

In the early days of non-organisation, everybody was a face or a potential face, but as the police became more organised so did the lads. In the old days, whether you were 30,000 or 3,000, the all-knowing hard-nut copper would be waiting for you on arrival.

'You think you're hard now, but later when the going gets tough you'll be glad we're here to take you back to your London train.' Sometimes the officer who said that had such conviction that you believed he really meant it and it wasn't just some throwaway line designed to wind you up, but usually they said it to let you know that he was on your case. I'm making this personal, TV style. If someone said something smart as they got off the train, like 'No need to push, officers – we're a football crowd, we do have some rights', they'd put their face an inch from yours so that you could smell what they had for dinner last night and growl: 'What did you say?' 'Nothing' was the answer they expected. Anything else usually meant a nicking. We were deluding ourselves anyway. We had no rights as football fans, so we made our own bill of rights and imposed it on everyone we came across.

The press wrote that we were all cowards who'd run to our mummies if we ever came up against a one-on-one fight. Some people believed everything they read, so one day at Bolton a Chelsea fan berated his mates when they chipped in with their boots on a Bolton fan caught on the wrong side of the station.

'Come on lads, I wanted to do him straight, man to man.'

'Bugger off, you dimwit, that only happens in the movies.'

You always got boys who just wanted to hang around the

periphery, to feel the adrenaline and get close to the buzz whilst keeping themselves well in check. They'd pretend to be game for any big event but kept close to the police escort, at the same time making all the noises that accompany a full marching away mob. They were face pickers who would pick someone out in the crowd across a fence and tell them they were going to cop it. 'Me and you mate. Over there in the car park. Away from the mob.' As if! Blond or ginger hair were favourites, and anyone wearing glasses was given a roasting. When they retaliated verbally, they were slaughtered. 'Fuck off, four-eyes, it's bad enough to wear bins without taking the piss with that double-glazing over the minces.' Mince pies: eyes. cockney rhyming slang. The boys loved to give it all that up north, especially to the Mancs and scousers.

Slap and move. That's it, keep moving, making yourself a harder target for the authorities. Yet always the police held the upper hand, because they knew where we were going and what made us tick. Deprive us of the match and they had won. The football was all we really wanted.

At the railway stations, the hard-core lads would slip away into smaller groups to look for their quarries, those who wanted the challenge. The days of massive battles across the roads and through town centres, conducted by hundreds of warring youths scattering the terrified, screaming shoppers (that was media talk, because mostly the shoppers took a step back then stood looking on perplexedly) were long gone. Only occasionally now would huge mobs clash, but the police would be briefed and waiting. If not, they were usually on the scene within minutes grabbing the first people they saw – the ubiquitous arrest for 'threatening words and behaviour'.

Vince Butler was once having a toe-to-toe with a Cardiff fan when in waded the police and grabbed him. Down at the station, the custody officer tried to get Vince to accept a charge of threatening words and behaviour.

'What for, I wasn't threatening anybody. This guy came along and hit me so I acted in self-defence. I was leathering seven bells out of him. If you lot hadn't turned up it would all have been settled man to man.'

'Look, if you accept a threatening words and behaviour charge you'll get a fine and be on your way.'

'No way, that's just to make your life easier, and I don't want a criminal record for nothing.'

'Assault it is then. How do you plead?'

'Not guilty. Self-defence.'

In front of a jury, Vince received his not guilty verdict. Meanwhile, all over the country fans were accepting the easy option. One Chelsea fan, a first-time offender, pleaded guilty to a threatening words and behaviour charge after making a stupid face at rival fans. He received seven days in jail.

Over the years, the fascination of football fans for trains grew. The lads travelled so much that football and diesel locomotives became welded together in everybody's mind. Flashing through all the different stations, Chelsea fans gained such an affinity with Kentish Town, Watford Junction, Corby and Crewe that we almost qualified to be train anoraks. Fans' conversations cross-referenced last week's violence on the terraces with the necessity to change trains twice and the time of the last train south from Crewe. Arsenal fans had the pleasure of being able to take the train out of King's Cross and watch it glide past their Highbury homes. I've never met anybody, young or old, who didn't get a lump in their throat when the underground emerged from the tunnels at Baker Street and they caught their first glimpse of Wembley's majestic white twin towers.

Arriving at the ground only to watch your team get stuffed out of sight and having to listen to the locals' mockery all the way home may be all pain and suffering, but getting there is as romantic as can be. England really is a green and pleasant land, even if the background canvas is painted in violent colours. It is no coincidence that one of the most romantic moments in cinematic history, in *Brief Encounter*, features a railway platform.

After the match, returning home again, the train became just another transportation vehicle, all dirty windows (if you got out of the local town without having your windows bricked in), unclean ashtrays, vomit, brown paint and chipped Formica tables – and that was when you won. After losing a match, especially an FA Cup match, the train felt like a travelling coffin, all rattle and roll with terrible silences relieved only by moans and shouts.

Then the coaches came along. No more train romance. Coaches were cheaper and more mobile. The coach signalled the beginning of the small mob confrontations. It suddenly became more personal.

FACES

YOU CAN'T PREDICT WHO'LL BECOME A FACE, it just happens, usually as a result of word of mouth amongst a person's peers. Hickey used to laugh at us in the early days, calling us 'the young mob'. Hickey laughed at everyone who had pretensions and tried to gain respect, but he never blanked any Chelsea fan. By now, Kojak was calling Hickey the main man, up there with Eccles and Babs. There were certain guys who felt they were above everybody else, and sneered at every firm except for those who were prepared to pay homage to their exploits. They never gained ultimate respect. Eccles, for all his nicknames and stories, never had the same aura as Hickey, because he only liked you if he decided you were part of what he wanted. He would organise, yet remained rather aloof, as if what he was doing was for himself rather than for the group, like a batsman who batted for himself first and the team second. His actions could win the match, but at the end of the day the glory was his to savour.

Porkies liked a kebab and though fat enough to be called Porkies, he wasn't large enough to get into the Brixton Bruisers mob. Incredible though it may seem, there really were young fans who felt that achieving a beer-and-kebab gut was something to be proud of. One day Porkies walked into the Black Bull with a group of his friends from the Leatherhead area. 'Is that Porkies' mob that's just walked in?' shouted Hickey across the bar, to much laughter from everyone else. The fact that they laughed meant that Porkies was becoming recognised although his mates, who had walked in with him, were mortified.

The older punchers didn't like us, because we had no respect for what had gone before. Who gave a toss that they'd taken the Bolton end in 1975? Many of the young dressers couldn't take them seriously because they had actually worn flares. As Giles said one day, 'They even wore donkey jackets with Irish company names on the backs. Come on, lads, is that low class or is that low class?'

We became faces without realising it. Whereas we used to follow others, it now dawned on us that people were following us, and had started asking us where the meeting place was and what was happening – get a load of that, Black Jim. After a while, you are deeply involved before you know it. As fans we shared everything: beer, cigarettes, programmes and stories, but mostly we shared the common bond of a love of our team and the shared experiences which bound us closer together. For many years, the biggest thing we shared was the disappointment of many false dawns which surrounded Chelsea.

When Hickey, Ginger Terry, Vince, Dougie and Dale went down in the Operation Own Goal trial, the press printed reams of garbage about the police undercover operation, overusing the word 'infiltration'. For a country brought up on a diet of American TV like *Hill Street Blues*, where the detectives dressed up as criminals to arrest drug addicts and gang members, it made wonderful copy. Reality, as usual, was completely different. Drugs officers can work undercover easily, because the only criterion is to be scruffy and smelly and have unwashed hair. All a drug addict is interested in is scoring the next fix; they would do a deal with the devil as long as they scored, but the infiltration of football fans is another matter. Everybody who goes to football has a history – it was the same for all the firms. Nobody ever appeared out of nowhere. Not once during his trial did the police ever claim to have been on Hickey's coaches, although he did once invite some uniforms on board for a return journey from Birmingham. 'Get on board, boys, we've got some great (blue) movies.' Considering that any group of fans could recognise their regional counterparts at 30 paces, it was comical to imagine that police officers could put on a Pringle sweater and suddenly become one of us. Leeds, Manchester United, Arsenal, Chelsea, West Ham, even Manchester City, all of them had some trademark, be it in their swagger, their overall dress code, or something intangible which made every group know who each was. Once in Turkey, in the Pudding Shop bar, a Chelsea fan astounded a group of backpackers when he pointed over at two lads who had just walked in: 'Look at those two. Definitely Leeds.'

There was also the question of allegiance to the team. A police officer couldn't have just gone to a match and pretended to be one of us, he'd have been spotted in seconds. Even if he could, he would have had to go so far undercover that he would have become one of us and that would have been the end of the operation. The police knew this, yet were happy for the press to tell an unsuspecting public that they'd infiltrated us. This led to a rumour alongside the theory that some of us were not really fans. Both myths ended up being debunked. Supporting your team is in the blood. It gets such a strong grip of you that reasoning and logic go out of the window, which is why the fighting madness sometimes descends and everybody flips once in a while.

The pub before the match was more than just a watering hole, a place to buy lager in short measures served in straight glasses – 'Serve me lager in a jug, barman. What do you think I am, some sort of poof?' – to be spilled as you fought your way back through the crowd to your place. It became part of the reason you went to

Chelsea. I have no doubt that it was the same for the pubs of every football fan up and down the country. Where you drank said as much about you as where you went inside the ground did. In the middle of the St Helier estate in south London, built after the war and one of the largest-ever council estates, was the St Helier Arms pub. The *Daily Mail* dubbed it the most dangerous pub in England after yet another shooting. The police had it closed down, arguing that the violent atmosphere of that pub wouldn't transfer to other ones, such was the creed of pub culture. Everybody thought their pub was the place to be. It might have dirty glasses, poor service, filthy toilets with no paper and be so crowded you'd get crushed half to death, but lads loved that pub like their own mothers. While it was bad being humiliated in the streets, there was always another chance to regain your reputation, but taking abuse from another mob while you stood doing nothing in your boozer was the ultimate in degradation. There was no return from that.

The Rose became an in-pub because it usually afforded a glimpse of the travelling fans arriving in the coach park. Untold would burst through the door of The Rose every Saturday there was a match on, his words echoing around the pub as others picked up his first line: 'There's untold of them around the corner.' Chaos is coming. With that, people would burst out of the pub and hurry along the road, usually returning a couple of minutes later denouncing it as an untold waste of time. Nobody cared, everyone laughed.

Those were the days before plain-clothes police officers, when every confrontation and battle could be relived across a flat pint of lager and nobody cared who heard. Not that the police would have learned anything. People only ever talked about the handbags-at-dawn type of confrontation. The really serious stuff was never boasted about. When the American ex-Marine Corps barman got glassed in Henry J. Beans, it made the national press who claimed the perpetrator was a scary fat man with frightening eyes. The general consensus around Chelsea was that the glass was in fact thrown by the girlfriend of one of the guys inside the bar. Also hardly mentioned was the rumour that the barman had been putting it about a bit and had slapped a couple of Chelsea fans for complaining the previous week.

There were unwritten rules of combat, which Chelsea certainly adhered to. If everybody were really as violent as the press said, it would have been easy to get a carload of lads and ambush certain known faces from the other mobs as they drank in their locals. Everyone knew who the main faces were. The rumour mill worked overtime and the Untolds of this world had a field day every Saturday, retelling what they'd heard. Denton had been slapped by the Spurs' main boys one evening in his Finsbury Park local. Sammy Skyves, a well-known Tottenham lad, sounded like a horizontal heavyweight, as there were so many stories doing the rounds about him getting a whacking. Jenkins had retired from the Arsenal scene because he had too many Spurs boys looking for him every Saturday night. Everybody listened intently and mulled the story over. Most rumours had a life of their own, and it just made you wonder who was around to witness these events.

Mickey Greenaway was probably the best-known name in London for a while. His reputation was so great that the media got to hear about him. Stories about his fighting prowess and leadership of Chelsea spread around England. That was no problem until you met Mickey and realised that he was just a fanatic whose love of Chelsea FC had become legendary. His only power lay in his voice. When he shouted 'Zigger Zagger', everybody heard it, including the opposing fans. At Chelsea, with the greyhound track stopping sound from carrying, that was some feat. In the days of 40,000 crowds, Mickey's 'Zigger Zagger' elicited a response from over 30,000 Chelsea boys. 'Oi Oi Oi,' they replied. Others tried to do the Zigger chant, but they were scorned. It was like Freddie and the Dreamers covering Beatles songs, it just wasn't done.

Eventually, the *Sunday People* told ten million readers that Mickey Greenaway was the King of the Soccer Hooligans. Even the police laughed at that one, but it reinforced the misconception that whatever was going on around football was organised, with leaders, infantry and organised battles. The press put it into context. Sure, there were people who could be considered organisers, generals or colonels-in-chief for the huddled masses, but Mickey wasn't one of them – he was 41, balding and a railway clerk who always wore a tie. This was the archetypal bogey man supposedly leading the line. Then, in the '70s, some writer wrote a novel about soccer hooligans containing every bad cliché there was, past, present and future, and the *Daily Express*, then the bible of the middle classes, serialised it. It sold ten copies and the author bought nine of them. Why read fiction when reality offered so much more?

Mickey Greenaway died in 1999. He was a legend at Chelsea, along with every player who has graced the turf in the past 30 years.

———

Top of the tree in London for a good few years were the West Ham boys. Like many Essex men who aspire to greatness, Bill Gardner moved into the leafy Surrey countryside of Reigate. He was wasted in football: his trademark introduction was more suited to the theatre: 'Good afternoon, my name is Bill Gardner,' he would say, 'and these are my ICF pals.' Bill would then whack someone and they would tear into each other, but most of all he loved to pose. 'Is he showing off his pecs, or what?' one of the Adelaide mob asked one day as Bill gave it his best muscular beach pose. Bill was a throwback to the '60s culture of Charles Atlas and the Dynamic Tension advert which promised to prevent nasty bullies kicking sand in your face. However, Bill and the ICF *were* the bullies depicted in the advert.

The walk from Upton Park tube is short in distance but high in stress. West Ham always frequented the market area and a little pub on the right-hand side, The Queens. Essex men and market traders, what a heady combination. It was a scriptwriter's dream, and would have made a great daily soap. Always standing around in Essex-man pose, the West Ham lads dared you to walk down that side of the road. Standing loud and proud across the width of the pavement, they would scan your face and body language as you neared them. Crossing over the road was a sure sign of fear, as if you were saluting their bravado.

They knew who you were the instant you walked out of the tube onto the High Road, even before you'd had the chance to scan the traffic. (Sometimes I think they knew who you were the moment you alighted from the tube – they could smell trepidation at 100 paces, but waited until they saw the whites of your eyes just to be sure.) The ticket area at the top of the exit steps within the station was too small to hang around in, but the market area 50 yards further down was their manor. 'You can hear the sound of Bow Bells from here,' they would sneer, then with a whack, 'Now they'll be ringing in your ear for the whole match.' Good afternoon indeed!

West Ham's finest hour at Chelsea came in September 1984. They had been hanging around the ground for hours before the match, slapping everybody they recognised. They were discerning, though, I'll give them that. When some Chelsea scarfers walked out of Parsons Green, spotted the West Ham boys then hesitated, turned and walked away, they shouted over to them, 'Don't worry. You're safe. We know who we're looking for.' Every time Chelsea mobbed up, they would appear somewhere unexpected, causing chaos. Towards the end of the match, which Chelsea won 3–0, two mobs appeared at each end of the Shed, scattering the terrace first one way then another, like an accordion being squeezed to the sound of their 'Bubbles' song. When Chelsea went back at them, they appeared somewhere else. On the Monday the press were evidently appalled, especially at the fans in the East Stand behind the press box, who were imploring the Chelsea Shed to 'get into 'em and damage those West Ham bastards'. When the Shed charged, the roars of approval from the East Stand caused frowns and head-shaking amongst the press.

Hickey's nicking and subsequent jailing was a massive downer.

People talked about Steve, Terry and Vince in hushed tones, while the Fulham mob pulled themselves together so tightly that even people who'd only been absent for a few games were asked where they'd been. Any new face was unwelcome, even if he had a history somewhere else. Even the guys who got off didn't like to shout about it. All of our worst nightmares came true, especially when Kevin went down for life and then Billy Mathews copped a four-year stretch. Stanley Alley looked like a picnic in comparison. I could just imagine the police aptitude test: 'How many different ways can you arrest and charge a football fan?' The charge sheets were piling up like dead Vietcong at Dien Bien Phu.

With West Ham coming up so fast, it didn't look like Chelsea could pull a proper firm together. After all, Hickey had been one of the main people, always coming out with stupid ideas. We all lost count of the number of times we'd sat in some obscure pub in Earls Court while Hickey told everyone to be patient because the other mob would be here soon. 'Trust me, boys, I run a courier business so I know the layout of these streets.' We all knew it was a load of tripe, yet we still sat there and listened. Hickey's daftest idea was to wait inside a gay pub at Earls Court because the police would never think of looking in there. When we turned up, the windows were blacked out so that nobody could see anything and the poofs looked bemused and perplexed. People drifted away while Hickey stood his ground, making everybody laugh because it had seemed like a good idea: 'So, what else would you be doing early on a Saturday evening?'

Occasionally, though, ambushes came off. The one on the High Street in Kensington when we ambushed the Everton was an original Hickey idea, and it worked to perfection. The scousers were owed that one if anybody was. Pimlico boys fired flare guns into the train carriage at point-blank range. Scousers lay on the floor begging for mercy: 'It wasn't us that cut up those lone cockneys and laughed about it, honest mate.'

'You're all innocent, of course. Anyway, have some for your guilty mates.' There wasn't a policeman in sight. The police came later and picked up the pieces, telling everyone they had it under control, they knew who the perpetrators were. But never once did the police try to infiltrate any groups, nor did they try to engage the young guys in conversation like they tried to do with Steve.

Chelsea had many different groups coming in from all over. Although we lacked any real organisation, people still turned up looking for a leader to follow. After Hickey went down, some clubs thought that they'd be able to come over and take liberties – they were mistaken. Adversity brought out the old faces.

Fat Chrissie Cresswell from Battersea was a 26-stone Colossus, part of a bunch of monsters known affectionately amongst us as the Brixton Bruiser Firm, which everybody said must be the heaviest mob in London. The lads reckoned they weighed in collectively at just over a ton. They remembered matches equally for the quality of the fight and the kebab that followed. Billy Matthews and Dave 'The Ox' Arden were part of the group.

They were big lumps, always getting stuck in but never running after or away from anybody. One day in the Swan, two lads were drinking and eating to excess. Their logic was that they would be better at scrapping like the Brixton Bruisers armed with a suitable belly. The fight had to be right in front of them and conducted at walking pace. 'We go through 'em, never at speed,' was their motto. The worse crime of all was a fight breaking out during feeding time, forcing them to throw their fast food at rival fans in order to get some punches in. 'Waste of good food, that.' They took X-rated retribution for that. They were great blokes to have around, unless you were picking up the restaurant tab or taking part in a McDonald's eating contest. One night Billy got a little too hungry on the bus going home to Wandsworth and bit someone's ear off, or so the prosecution alleged at his trail when they arrested him over a year after the offence was committed. By the time Billy got jailed, nobody on the street could tell fact from fiction, as the press were out of control.

Action often happens when you least expect it, especially when West Ham's involved. The following season the Chelsea boys decided to meet early one morning, around 9 a.m., then travel out to east London and ambush the West Ham boys coming in on the district line. Leaflets had been printed, although most people spread information by word of mouth. The 9 a.m. meet was for breakfast upstairs in the Black Bull. It was to be strictly liquid of course. It's a crime in itself to be in a pub at that time and be seen eating! As myself and Stuart walked up the road from Fulham Broadway, there was already a crowd hanging around outside. We walked past the Rising Sun opposite the Shed end, and at 20 paces had to get on our toes as we realised it was West Ham.

'What's up with those bastards, can't they sleep?' shouted Giles at me.

Further back down the road, Nashy and around 30 of the boys were milling around. They too had been caught unawares by the sudden appearance of 50 to 80 West Ham boys. They had stopped running by now and were walking towards us waving their arms. 'Look at them wankers doing the West Ham walk,' muttered Nashy. 'What time's take-off, they're flapping like ducks,' muttered someone else, causing ripples of nervous laughter. We saw it as a variation on the Lambeth Walk and the West Ham boys had it off pat.

Everybody stopped. The West Ham mob was still walking slowly forward. Gingermop Gardner was to the fore, along with all their main faces. Even at a distance we could see those grins. 'What is it they have down there, grinners' disease?' asked Jason, one of Nashy's mob. It was the humour which stems from nervousness before an off. Suddenly everyone heard the electrical whine of a milk float glide past at walking pace. The milkman was whistling, oblivious of the forthcoming mayhem. Everybody looked at each other and grinned. 'Good morning, here's my early morning milk order,' said Porkies. Without a word, four or five of us ran forward and grabbed a full crate. 'Oi, what the hell do you think you're doing?' shouted the milkman. He then made the fatal error of stopping and getting off. By the time he got back on his float, most of his milk had been unloaded. 'Too late, mate, I hope our credit's good.'

'Breakfast's on me, Gardner,' shouted Kenny as the first bottle spun through the air, exploding at their feet. Within seconds, the West Ham were retreating under a hail of milk bottles as hundreds smashed on and around them. Go back in time a few winters and this was a bunch of schoolboys having a snowball fight. When a bottle exploded on the back of one fan, a huge collective cheer went up. The picture on the faces of the Chelsea boys was one of pure joy. The barrage went on for a minute or two until the lads ran out of ammunition. The milkman was nowhere to be seen. His empty milk float looked a strange sight surrounded by an ocean of empty red crates, smashed bottles and a puddle of milk caused by our frantic desire to grab another bottle. Further up the road was a mountain of glass and a river of milk. Beyond it were the glum faces of the West Ham.

If Southall was Calcutta then Aston Villa was Bombay, no doubt about it. There was row after row of Asian shops with meat sitting in unrefrigerated windows next to magazines and newspapers: I'll have a *Sun* and some salmonella, please. The whole place stank of curry as you walked past. The state of the place! What is it about areas like that? They always seem to be full of litter and other rubbish. Chelsea lads who were not National Front certainly listened to those who were talking about the corruption of England and the dilution of the English national identity after a trip to Villa. Witton, Sparkbrook, and the surrounding areas didn't seem English at all. You were suddenly in a place you didn't belong, but not like those parts of Liverpool or Manchester where human beings were living degraded, poverty-stricken existences. This was something else – it wasn't threatening, it just enveloped you. Brown faces looked at you from behind grimy net curtains or dirty shop windows as you walked past, yet you never saw one of them amongst the Villa mob. All good Villa boys loved their Holte End.

Chelsea were down, relegated out of the top league once again.

Hickey and the rest of the coach lads handed out leaflets: 'Travel on Hickey's coach. Sod relegation. Get drunk and enjoy yourself. 28th April 1979. 1st stop Lewisham 8.10 a.m.' Outside the ground, the police were in a particularly mocking mood. 'I don't know why you lot bothered turning up, you're already relegated. Ha ha.' They were safe in the knowledge that they wouldn't be seeing our ugly mugs next season, until Chelsea scattered the Holte End good and proper, turning their smug looks to panic. Hickey made the words into an infamous chant by repeating them over and over again on the coach microphone, all the way back down the M1.

Politicians dismissed us as a minority staining the national character. We couldn't be ignored that easily, though, because throughout the 20-year period of front page headlines, the public derived a voyeuristic pleasure bordering on sadism from reading about our exploits. Anyone who says that they didn't get a kick from reading those stories is a liar. Sunday breakfast for most people wouldn't have been the same without page after page of reports of crowd violence. At Heysel, the cameras filmed the charge by the Liverpool fans then stayed on and focused on the fighting. There were plenty of Alf Garnett types out there watching the TV, cheering on the English lads and cracking the Italian retreat jokes long before Liverpool fans charged and a wall collapsed. When it was decided by the press that what had happened was terrible, these people threw up their arms crying out that hooliganism had to be stopped once and for all.

The public dramatisation of the ritual of football violence made us seem exciting. The terraces gave us the chance to feel something more and to attain greatness, even if the words used to describe us were all culled from the same thesaurus – everybody called us animals. None of that mattered, because we were different. In a nondescript world sanitised by mass advertising, we'd developed our own culture and form of expression and we were frightening the rest of them to death.

If the politicians had wanted to, they could have looked at the causes of what we were doing and worked out some solutions and saved themselves years of grief, long before mass-hooliganism died of its own accord. (There was in fact a theory that it was dying out as early as 1979. Nobody wanted to read that sort of thing, preferring the lurid headlines, proof that there was a greater evil at play than lads enjoying the confrontation.) The same politicians who were executive directors of numerous companies hadn't heard of trends and product life cycles when it came to hooligans. By the time the mass battles died out because everybody from the hooligan generation had got old, the politicians had given us crowd barriers, resulting in the tragic deaths at Hillsborough. They had also mustered up the police National Intelligence Unit, which cost hundreds of thousands of pounds, yet couldn't gather enough intelligence to stop a drunken outbreak of fighting in Marseilles, in the 1998 World Cup.

People began asking themselves what the politicians really wanted, and what sort of advisers they were using. Take the guys at Loughborough University, who got financial grants to research the scourge of hooliganism. John Williams, an academic, once stated on TV: 'English people love to fight,' and 'Young Englishmen think that it is good to fight.' For the price of a pint you could have got that from Scarrott, without all the long-winded explanations and subjunctive clauses. When your living depends on people paying you to make those sort of conclusions, why on earth would they say it was dying and lose their funding?

It was the same with everything associated with football hooliganism. It became a cottage industry, totally reliant on violence spontaneously erupting every so often. Even now, the press tell us that it isn't really dead, only hibernating. Spooky isn't the word for the parasitic urges these hangers-on must have. The media had the power to make people famous and many loved the chance to be in the limelight.

The emergence of football youth culture undoubtedly spawned a whole new industry. Sociologists, people watchers, Uncle Tom Cobley and all had a view on it. Even the *Readers Digest* condensed our behaviour for the American readers. 'TIME

TO BLOW THE WHISTLE ON HOOLIGANS', it wrote, then gave the game away about the credibility of their utterances:

> Luton Town, March 14, 1985. A mob of hooligan cut-throats rampages through the stands and invades the pitch during an FA Cup match, cracking skulls and belting police with bottles, darts and splintered seats. Afterwards, Millwall supporters sweep through the terrorised town, smashing shop fronts throwing cars on to their sides, and lastly destroying the train taking them home.

They forgot to explain how the lads actually got home after they had destroyed the train.

'Mobs of hooligan cut-throats.' For a while, everybody was sitting in Bleak House reciting Dickens. Some of the things written over the years defied description, yet this could have topped any list of incredible utterings. They said we did it because we were politically disenfranchised. Most of the boys didn't have a clue what that meant. 'Disenfranchised, mate? I've got a foreskin.' The *Mail on Sunday* asked influential intellectuals for their solutions. Amongst the ban, flog and jail 'em comments were two classics. Monic Mason, assistant to the director of the Royal Ballet, said: 'Are football hooligans that bad at 7.30 a.m.? Football matches should be played before breakfast.' The best came from David Wall, director of the Royal Academy of Dancing: 'Make the physical discipline of ballet compulsory in schools, and the yobs will be too tired to make trouble.' Nobody told that to Steve Scully from Twickenham when he launched his infamous Chelsea kung fu kick against Crystal Palace in a cup match in 1975. It was delivered with an aggressively graceful movement of which Rudolph Nureyev would have been proud.

There was always plenty of humour from the lads, laughing at descriptions of the havoc they had caused. In Euro '88 in Germany many years later, some middle-aged Man U boys told an ageing SS officer they were drinking with that they had achieved what Adolf Hitler never could in his blitz – their blitzkrieg Red Army had shut down the London Underground.

The rest of the world, watching us on the TV news, didn't understand where we were coming from. The dumb shits took it to heart. Writers took on the mantle of historians, not realising that they were witnessing history being made in front of their very eyes.

What made Thatcher's blood boil, and probably frightened her the most, was seeing the symbols of order, which she so loved, retreating in their blue uniforms under a hail of plastic seats thrown like frisbees by lads running across the pitch at Luton laughing and shoving each other. They could have been throwing snowballs at their primary school teacher, only now they were older, stronger and on a different playground. It was a laugh, all the fun of the fair, nothing more – couldn't they see that? We certainly could. Plastic seats whizzed through the air, each one a toy aeroplane. When hundreds were flying, the police retreated to a chant of 'BACK BACK BACK'. At Portsmouth, the police retreated and stood back until the boys ran out of seats. Then some wag shouted, 'Sit down, you lot.' Ken Bates came over to the Chelsea boys with a stern warning. 'Behave, you lot, or I'll sell Kerry Dixon to Arsenal.' Now that really was a threat to us. Dixon was our hero, tall, blond, and scoring goals aplenty. One time he scored at Manchester United just as we were scattering the Stretford End. He looked up at the parting of the red sea, half-thinking that he was responsible for it.

Thatcher demanded action, then appointed a Minister for Sport: Colin Moynihan was his name. With his red hair, he looked like a miniature Bill Gardner. All the Chelsea boys had a good laugh about that, mocking Moynihan and Bill in the pub. Meanwhile, Moynihan promised action on every front. No politician ever missed the chance in those years to indulge in English military metaphors. His every announcement was greeted with dismay. Eventually, the cynical media dubbed him stupid. When England played in Poland, Moynihan decided that England fans would not be sold tickets, but the lads got their revenge: 2,000 England fans turned up and gained entry. We mocked him in a series of postcards, one of which was printed in *The Mail on Sunday*.

> Maggie's Puppet – You know you will never stop us pip-squeak. Here we are in Warsaw having a ball. Where are you? Watching rugby? Or maybe Maggie hasn't let you out of the closet!! HERE WE ARE AGAIN CHEL3EA HEADHUNTERS.

Moynihan said: 'It's a sad reflection on a long-running and mindless hate and smear campaign. Once again, it takes a sick mind to send abuse on an Auschwitz postcard. There are no limits to the depths some of these so-called football fans will sink.'

Nothing racist or anti-semitic was meant by the use of an Auschwitz card. It seemed apt and funny, but the press turned it round again.

The scousers were reckoned to be the best thieves, scroungers or 'jibbers' as they called themselves, but the Chelsea boys had some excellent characters in their ranks. Thieving was considered to be a good profession amongst the lads, especially those stealing from rich people. Not for nothing is Arthur Daley a well-loved London character. Whatever the London boys did, it was always done with style. Topper from Northolt, who had a short, neat hairstyle going slightly bald on top, always had a tidy little firm with him. He was always wedged up, with at least a monkey in the back pocket. Topper was one of the first to go robbing in Europe. Switzerland might have been the land of cuckoo clocks, but to him it was Rolexville. A man ahead of his time and top geezer, hence the nickname. People would nod towards his crew: 'Great shoppers, that lot.' Chelsea boys didn't go thieving, they went shopping. By 1999 shopping had become recognised as a leisure industry. Topper and the boys were 15 years ahead of their time on that one. They were always going abroad and coming back with nice watches and other stuff. Their favourite line was: 'Only we can steal to order. Eighteen-carat belcher chains our speciality.' Once they were asked if they would take a cheque for a beautiful-looking Raymond Weil watch, for which they were asking a double ton. Topper looked at the fellow, then held up the chequebook he had pulled out for ridicule. 'A cheque, you dozy bastard? I'm offering you a Raymond Weil, direct from Geneva. Swiss fucking precision, you can time your wanking by the second, it's not some fucking plastic cuckoo clock. Your first quality watch since your Timex broke and you want to offer me a cheque? I don't even wear checked shirts.'

Another serial thief was Winkle, who was a legend around Chelsea. Only ever dressed in jeans and trainers, he was skinny with mousey hair and was always trying to sell you something in the pub before football. He was an unbelievable shoplifter with the fastest hands you'd ever seen, and eyes that never stopped moving on top of his twitchy head. He was looking around, casing and pricing up his next dodgy enterprise, turning up in the pubs flogging bent gear. Winkle never stopped ducking and diving, and was either returning from or planning his next robbery. 'Sometimes football interrupts my thieving. One's gotta go,' he would muse over a pint. Then, inevitably: 'Nah, I can definitely manage both.'

We heard stories that his little burglary gang stopped climbing up drainpipes and developed a new approach to gain entry – they would knock on the front doors of the big houses in Chelsea with a sledgehammer, saying, 'Pardon me, rich blokes, this is the Cheyne Walk Choo Choo,' and then just walk in during broad daylight and help themselves. 'Nobody puts a burglar alarm on during the day when the servants are in the house, do they? All you ever come across are the posh Norland nanny in her silly green uniform and a few underpaid Filipinos doing the ironing and housework. What do they expect, living in a £1 million house on four floors and never being there because they're working in the City?' explained Winkle ever so matter-of-factly one day over a pint.

One day he disappeared from the scene, and all that remained were the rumours. He was shot for doing a villain's house. We knew he was asthmatic – maybe he'd been nicked and had had a bad athsma attack in Fulham police station, then died later in hospital? Others claimed that he was doing a ten-year stretch and had expired in the nick. Someone else said he'd retired to Tenerife to help his athsma and was robbing timeshares. After all, he once said, 'I might have to move to Tenerife because there's 26 new customers in each apartment every year.' No one ever got to the bottom of the story, he just became an absent face whose exploits made us laugh when we reminisced. A dead legend.

Then the 'Boro lot came on the scene, machine freaks, led by Leggy Gibbon and Jock. One of them had learned how to open up gaming machines using a screwdriver. They could get the machine to go into automatic payout, or they would just smash open the bottom lock and clean out all the money below, tokens and all. Like the wheel changers at a motor-racing Grand Prix, they were in and gone in little over six to ten seconds. Once at an away game they cleared over £250 of 50p pieces during the coach journey stops. Someone got hold of the bag and started throwing them around the coach – pretty soon the floor was covered in them. The boys' protestations about lack of respect for hard-earned cash fell on deaf ears.

With the pubs packed to the rafters, it was easy for them to operate in and around football grounds. They didn't stand on ceremony and if any London team were playing at home, they would go around and do the pubs in the evening, right in front of the home or away fans. It was strictly business, and their front was immense. Nobody ever stopped them.

They also made up plastic strimmers which imitated 50p pieces, and used them to knock up £30 worth of credits, then they'd take the payout.

Hanging around with dodgy geezers like that, as if we were moving in a parallel universe to the rest of society, was all part of the attraction of our culture, and added to our mystique. It was a sort of *Clockwork Orange* existence except that we didn't have a different language – apart, of course, from the slang words which came along. One day Winkle came into the Black Bull and said: 'Want to see some dodgy tom?' Some of the lads thought he meant he had a prostitute somewhere, whereas he really meant 'tomfoolery' (rhymes with jewellery).

No pre-match drink was complete without Brains from Lewisham turning up with his magic carrier bag. Wherever he went, he had it with him. Whether it was Liverpool, Manchester or Birmingham, you'd see him walking down the road with his carrier bag. It was never the same one mind you, but always different, Tesco or Sainsbury. Never Harrod's, though; he drew the line at that. 'What's in it?' everybody used to ask. 'Mind your own business,' was his stern reply. The police would stop and ask to see in it sometimes, so he'd open it for them then immediately shut it. Nobody ever found out what he had in that bag. It was one of life's little mysteries.

Skitzy, a real character, was a lifeguard at Lewisham baths. Over the years he appeared on most people's coaches and was universally well liked, which is unusual because there is always somebody somewhere who doesn't like so-and-so. The last I heard of him he was a doorman at the Lazy Toad in Beckenham.

There was a Chelsea fan called Avis, who used to drink in the Man in the Moon pub. Always wearing a baseball cap, he used to stand at the bar with his pit-bull terrier, Buster. One day, he walked out and bumped into a bunch of cockney Red Mancs who nicked his Fila cap. With that, he picked up his pit-bull and ran at them. The dog was going berserk, and they stopped in their tracks, threw his cap back to him and ran away. It must have upset the dog, because when the match was over someone stepped on his paw and he sank his teeth into the guy's leg. It took them ten minutes to prise his jaws apart.

Tweedy was a ticket tout over at Chelsea, who always had serious money on him. The boys loved hearing stories about the wedged-up lads travelling up north and going into some obscure pub, pulling out a huge wad of cash, then buying a 40-quid round and seeing the landlord's startled expression. When Chelsea played at Sunderland, he organised the away trip via Concorde. Those who didn't know him pooh-poohed it and wouldn't believe he'd really done such a thing, but were forced to admit he had when the BBC showed a documentary about Concorde, and Tweedy's smiling mug was on display. Real class.

––––––––––––

Pretty soon, the cult of football was surrounded by people who were attracted to the thrill of the firm. For years the scousers of Liverpool and Everton had teamed up as one mob and Chelsea, with their reputation for violence, attracted some hangers-on – it became a badge of honour to say that you'd fought with Chelsea at Leeds. Fat Pat and his ilk loved to put out the word that they were in with the main faces of various firms. Then there were ponces like McGregor, who would earwig different conversations then spread the news, which caused trouble with many firms (although never with West Ham, they didn't tolerate crap like that). There were many who wondered what the hell McGregor, who was QPR, was doing coming along to Chelsea. The Headhunters didn't like him and kept him at arm's length, although it was rumoured that he had once bossed some of the boys in a skirmish with the Gooners and that he had also tried it at a Forest away game. As far as we were concerned he was an interloper. After all, we had to be there – we were Chelsea, it was our team, but what was he doing? Getting off on it? Strutting with the big boys? If he'd wanted, he could have tried to put together a little firm.

Then one day came the ultimate insult – QPR put on a show against Chelsea. In amongst depressing high-rise flats and litter-strewn gardens, where even the dogs jumped the fences to shit in the street, was Loftus Road, QPR's ground. When Chelsea walked down there, Munday pulled a huge blade and backed us off, then stood in the road outside an ugly looking pub in the South Africa Road, offering it about. It was a few seconds before Chelsea were going back at him. Then the Old Bill turned up and the blade disappeared, but with the police there he had protection and was able to shout his mouth off. By this time the police were really in charge, with dogs, helicopters and so many vanloads of Plod that the crime rate must have been rocketing elsewhere in London (it was). Despite the police, Chelsea retaliated and charged at the QPR, scattering them. The police lined us up and the little prat walked alongside gloating: 'I see you've been done again, Chelsea.'

Some of the lads badly wanted to do him and went looking for him for a few weeks. Eventually tempers cooled, but he knew he wasn't welcome in certain parts of Chelsea after that and kept a low profile. Sure, some Chelsea lads went down to Fulham because they were born there, but our lot didn't follow other teams. Only nonentities did that.

———

From the beginning the press were our constant companions, hasty scribblers or dedicated cameramen. In the days before mobile video cameras, the only records of the action were the black-and-white stills that decorated every Sunday newspaper and then our bedroom walls. Those were the days when getting nicked was something to laugh about down the pub. The madness and the bitterness were a part of it as well, but we were into it, enjoyed it. Sometimes you'd look at the press and sneer at them. They needed us but we didn't need them, except to boost our own egos. Some of the lads hated them, and took every opportunity to dish them out a dig when they got the chance. Mostly, though, the press were ubiquitous in the same way as rats are always around humans. It didn't matter what you did, they never went away. But they never learnt anything of substance from any football fan, because all their quotes were one-liners. 'We done 'em', 'We run 'em', or 'We're the hardest'. It was primary school playground talk, and every week they made more of it than anybody could have imagined. They made us famous, yet none of the writers or photographers made their careers out of it, or became famous themselves. No Don McCullum or Lord

Lichfield followed us around. Guys talked about buying a camera and really telling a story, and what a story that would have been. An Arsenal lad was once spotted with a Smart Canon with plenty of lens attachments, but I never saw any of his work published.

The police became faces in their own right. Everybody recognised the dodgy coppers, by reputation if not by sight. Stories about good and bad coppers were as prolific as the police themselves. Sometimes there were so many of them that it made you wonder where they all came from.

We all had at least one incredible copper story. These were fishermen's tales, not about the one that got away, but about the night we got away with something.

'Outside Victoria, about 30 of us. Up comes a police inspector. "Listen, lads," he says, "the Everton are due here in a few minutes and they beat up one of our officers a few weeks ago. You've got two minutes to do your worst before we turn up. No innocent bystanders, women or children. Otherwise the Everton are all yours. Then make yourselves scarce so that we can nick a few."'

The best story was about the famous Arsenal match night when Miller's firm chased Chelsea across Highbury Fields and in the chaos ran Chelsea from pillar to post. 'I'm telling you, lads, this copper pulls out a truncheon and goes into the Arsenal boys like a raving lunatic, hitting them with his truncheon in one hand and his helmet in the other, shouting at them all the while: "You ain't doing my Chelsea boys, I'm Chelsea too. Do them and you do me."'

The only tall tale we ever gave credence to, because we were there, was the time in Manchester when a vanload of white coppers pulled up and told a massive Chelsea mob that Mickey Francis and his merry men were around the corner at a chip shop, awaiting our pleasure. It was well known that Mickey had set up his little mob on racial lines, and the white Manchester police officers didn't like that whole Moss Side thing, which had been exacerbated by the riots in June 1981. At their request, we had a livener with Mickey and his boys, although there were a few white boys with them. They all had it on their toes. Mickey, with his Moss Side mentality (every fan thinks that their firm comes from the roughest part of Britain, even plonkers from Oxford), went on about white boys being frightened of blacks – well, I reckon his firm were petrified of Chelsea that day.

The police in Liverpool believed they were the main faces at Anfield, they weren't going to let us cocky Chelsea fans come up and strut it on their turf. Arriving at Lime Street, some know-it-all sergeant would say: 'You're gonna wear it today, lads, the Everton and Liverpool have teamed up to give it to you.'

'You'd better open up extra casualty wards to put them all in then,' we'd retort.

Scousers called the police 'the busys' with a modicum of fear. They never got to grips with the fact that we could swagger across Stanley Park and hold our own on it. Instead, they attacked us the only way they knew how – Liverpool police telling us they weren't going to let us in to sit in the seats we'd purchased.

One copper, Sergeant Hobbs, became our soulmate; he knew us by name. Some of the lads joked that they saw more of Hobbs than they did of their girlfriends. Perhaps we should have given him a nickname. One day in December 1988, at a Spurs game, I had been hanging around outside the turnstiles waiting for the Spurs mob. No sooner had I gone in to catch the kick-off, thinking that they weren't going to show, than the Spurs boys turned up looking for aggro. The police shut the big metal railings to stop everyone from spilling out onto the road and through them I could hear the unmistakable noise of people running everywhere in chaos. Hobbs saw me through the fence.

'You should be out here, Henderson, this is where the action is,' he grinned.

The police jailed a lot of people, but that didn't mean they were all guilty or criminal acts had been committed. Consequently, it meant nothing. As fast as people went down, football violence seemed to escalate. You could imagine the police chief sitting in his gleaming chrome tower looking out over London on a Saturday afternoon, briefing his men. 'Somewhere out there are hard-core football hooligans, all looking for the giant row in which we can nick them good and proper. Please, God, just once.'

All the far-right conspiracy theories which the press loved to invent were ended on a June evening in 1988 outside Dusseldorf station when German skinheads and English lads, rumoured to be neo-Nazis together, battled it out across town, squirting each other with CS gas. Only a few months previously the media had told the public that the far-right contingent would be teaming up in Germany, forming a hooligan alliance. When Combat 18 (the numbers represented the letters A and H in Adolf Hitler's name) was formed in 1992, it was supposed to have active members at Chelsea, but nobody sat there talking about politics in the pub. Most of the chat was banter and piss-take. Who had time for politics? That was a fad. Undoubtedly some did, and there were active Combat 18 members at Chelsea, but the talk of politics would dissipate as fast as it took Untold to say his famous six words. Other clubs, such as Leeds, were far more racist than Chelsea. Charlie Sargent was known as an important figure in the BM. He came along to Chelsea matches, although he was an Arsenal fan, and England matches. He talked about the English nationality. There's nothing new in that, so does everybody, but his views were too extreme to laugh about.

People dressed in Hitler masks and gave Nazi salutes to shock. Britain beat the Germans in two world wars and a world cup. They were hardly going to seriously imitate such losers. Not that the Nazi thing didn't get a few laughs.

In the late '70s, Chelsea played Cambridge United. Cambridge were basically a non-league team who had managed to climb to the dizzy heights of the second division. Consequently, their ground was rubbish. The local police didn't have a clue what was descending on them when we arrived. In the town was a fancy-dress shop and in it were loads of Hitler masks, no doubt worn for fun by the Cambridge undergraduates, destined to become the ruling class, at their fancy-dress balls. The lads raided the shop, so inside the ground there were tons of people wearing Hitler masks.

At the away end, the police had rigged up an observation tower on some scaffolding. The Chelsea boys got bored with the match and started rocking the tower, with the police inside. They leaned over. 'Stop that, you lot,' one said in an authoritative voice, as if his gravitas would deter us.

That spurred the crowd on even more. A song went up. Rock-abye baby, in the treetops. By now, an old stern-voiced policeman was begging us to stop, along with the other policemen up there. 'Please, lads.' Eventually, they negotiated their way down. Chelsea won the match quite easily. The next day, a picture of fans in Hitler masks was shown under the caption: 'Chelsea fans salute their team after their victory'.

At a Preston away game the curse of Hitler struck again with a mob turning up wearing deely bopper headgear with springs, which usually had balls on the end. Some wag had had loads made with swastikas on them. Looking back now it seems stupid, but at the time, when 50 guys wearing them appeared in the Preston end, it seemed like the funniest thing we'd ever seen. As fighting erupted, all you could make out were these swastikas bouncing around. Even some of the policemen were laughing. Eventually, the police led the idiots out and walked them around the pitch. As they got to the halfway line, some older fans started remonstrating with them about their headgear. One of the fans jumped into the crowd, others followed, and another fight broke out. Standing no more than five feet away was Nobby Stiles. One old Preston boy leant over. 'Do you know who that is? That's Nobby Stiles, hero of England's greatest victory over Germany.'

'Fuck him,' shouted one of the Chelsea boys, 'Let's get into him as well.' There was then the undignified sight of Nobby, the scourge of Germany in 1966, getting on his toes for a few yards while some idiot with a swastika on a spring bouncing around his head went at him. The voice of reason prevailed and another Chelsea fan grabbed him. 'Leave it out – that's Nobby, he really was a hero.' Poor Nobby looked terrified, hero or not.

Basically, we were patriots. In Stockholm a group of us were drinking in the King's Head. At nearly three times the cost of the English equivalent for a pint, nearly anything else seemed like a good idea. When somebody produced a map and exclaimed that the Argentine Embassy was just around the corner, we decided to decamp there to tell the Argies that the Falklands were British and would always remain so. That was nothing compared to the best political protest I ever saw a group of football fans make.

Chelsea had played Manchester City at home. Everyone had congregated in the Nell Gwynn pub after the match, but the coaches were being well guarded and no Manchester guvnors had dared to show – nothing new there. Then Hickey, who loved a speech, informed the pub that Chelsea had to uphold the honour of England by marching on the Iranian Embassy, where the famous siege was going on. Led by General Hickey the boys marched across Hyde Park Corner, arriving outside the Iranian embassy to be confronted by hundreds of Iranians praying to Mecca. Forward went the 200 and charged gloriously, scattering them, and leaving bemused police officers looking at a large number of Iranians sprawled across the tarmac, wondering what had hit them. Two days later the SAS, inspired by Hickey, stormed the embassy. The Chelsea fans' charge was caught on film and ended up in a musical montage, recorded for posterity on the BBC's *Rock and Roll Years*.

Being a face carried responsibilities with it. You were no longer just another anonymous person, you represented the whole creed of the support. Your actions determined the level of respect people had for your team. One night in Liverpool, the lads got caned. Some of the older boys lost it completely and ran past the younger ones who tried to hold it together. 'Don't run,' they shouted. 'Fuck you,' was the undignified reply and they all tore off together.

Worse than anything was seeing a picture of yourself in full flight in the Sunday papers. For those who had lost it, thoughts of 'what if' constantly lingered in the back of their minds. 'I panicked and started to run, not knowing what I was doing,' they would always say with a distant, almost dead, look in their eyes.

'Nobody blames you,' their friends would say, but someone somewhere always did.

NATIONAL PRIDE

'ABROAD IS BLOODY' – GEORGE V

Chelsea were big on the England scene. Some said Chelsea followed England because they were so bad that they couldn't get into Europe, but the real reason was simple – it was great fun. Twenty-four-hour drinking and foreign trips with your mates. Nothing much had changed since D.H. Lawrence wrote this on 18 August 1914:

> The reservists were leaving for London by the nine o'clock train. They were young men, some of them drunk. There was one bawling and brawling before the ticket window; there were two swaying on the steps of the subway shouting, and ending, 'Let's go and have another before we go.' There were a few seeing off their brothers, but on the whole the reservists only had their own pals.
> 'Well, so long!' they cried as the train began to move. 'When you see 'em, let 'em have it.'
> 'Ay, no fear,' shouted the man, and the train was gone, the man grinning.
> I thought what it would really be like, 'when he saw 'em'.

In the early 1980s it was common to see loads of England lads dressed in dark-blue Admiral tops. Admiral were the England team's sponsor at the time. With the three stripes, it could have been a contingent of sailors direct from HMS *Invincible*. Instead, the lucky foreigners had an undisciplined rabble letting them have it whenever they saw them.

Without doubt, the benchmark for foreign travel was the France v England friendly match played in March 1984. The fighting started with the French skinheads on the Paris métro, where both sides had armed themselves with CS gas, and continued throughout the match with seats being smashed all around. As the Paris riot police came through the crowd, Paul Penny from Kilburn skimmed seats into the front row of the riot police like frisbees. They bounced off the front of their protective clothing, hardly even making an impression, yet every time one connected people cheered. At the fairground, for such accuracy, he would have won a whole row of cuddly toys but for his trouble that night he got a good whacking with a police truncheon.

At Dunkirk, some of the lads disembarked from the ferry to find rows of brand-new British Leyland cars ready for export on the quayside, complete with ignition keys. An impromptu game of bumper cars ensued in front of startled, open-mouthed French onlookers. British Leyland estimated the damage at £30,000.

Another landmark match was Denmark away in 1982. Copenhagen is a wonderful city, full of gentle Danes offering you polite advice and friendship – unless you are a travelling England fan. The local youths want to pick a fight, like they do everywhere. One of the lads walked out of a Copenhagen bar to a smack in the teeth: 'They don't print that in the guidebooks, do they!' Everywhere you go, English fans set the standards for toughness. Mix it with us and you've got credibility. A smack in the teeth doesn't need translation, it's a universal language.

Guppy from Brighton loved Copenhagen until he stepped in the dog shit which seemed to be everywhere. 'Wonderful, Wonderful Copenhagen Your Streets Are Full of Shit' became his theme tune after that.

Inside the ground, the local police hadn't heard of segregation and fight after fight broke out. The locals were up for it. In fact, they were thriving on it. Plain-clothes policemen mingled with them and got stuck in because it was fun, like a boxing booth at a travelling fairground. For a short while, one end of the ground resembled a punch-in-the face contest.

In one comical exchange, two large coppers in plain clothes set about an England fan near the front. Hickey charged down the terracing and delivered a kung fu kick which sent the larger, blond-haired policeman bouncing against a fence. The momentum knocked Hickey to the ground. Another police officer stepped forward and lashed him with his truncheon around 20 times. The riot police snatch squad arrived and the two policemen flashed their badges at them, so they proceeded to give Hickey a good bashing. As he got up to run away, blondie gave him a beauty of a punch to the side of his head which knocked him sideways, then sent him on his way with a kick up the backside. Everyone laughed, especially when he retreated up the terrace still getting a whacking from the retreating police. The wind was knocked from his body, but he was half-laughing at his escape from Thumpsville and at everyone's incredulity at his stupid bravery. 'Just my luck to pick on the police.'

The two plain-clothes policemen were now unmasked. Instead of melting away, they stood there like latter-day John L. Sullivans in the classic old boxers' pose: both arms out in front moving up and down, while slightly bouncing on the spot. 'Come forward, English hooligans, we are ready to fight.' Very politically correct, very Danish. Forward went the lads, ready to take up the challenge, but there was a very polite afterthought which the Danes had conveniently left out: 'We are offering you a fight which we cannot lose. If you beat us in a fight we will have you nicked and battered by our best riot police, not necessarily in that order, Mr Englishman.' Hickey had found that out the hard way!

All the while, this was going on to a backdrop of thousands of Danes singing a happy oompah song while they swayed from side to side in unison. When the huge blond copper took a particularly good right-hander and staggered backwards, the Danish crowd let out a huge 'ooh' roar, swayed at a higher speed and sang a little louder. Oh, what fun these English hooligans are providing us with. Afterwards, in a bar on the Nyhaun, the Danish equivalent of Covent Garden: 'We really love you English hooligans. You certainly know how to have a fine punch-up.'

Seems that the police getting a whacking is popular wherever you go. Leaving Copenhagen station the next day, the locals and police waved goodbye. 'Come back again, boys.' Unreal.

Denmark '88 was just as much fun. The only difference was the level of organisation we needed in order to keep away from the police. By now, the police were using the press as a propaganda weapon, telling the public that they had circulated details of the hooligans to all Danish airports so that all known troublemakers would be denied entry. Despite being told that for years, I never knew of anybody who had been denied entry to a country. Scarrott used to get off his face at Dover and continue to drink on the ferry and train until he arrived at his continental destination, but was never once refused entry. Okay, so he used a false passport, but using the names Elvis Presley and Al Capone, amongst other aliases, should have alerted a criminal intelligence unit.

Anyway, the lads all met in the centre of Hamburg. Neo-Nazis or not, the local pimps and rougher class who hang around the red light district, the Reeperbahn, soon came into conflict with us. In the centre of the Reeperbahn there was a series of bars where the local black population hung out. On the Monday evening, Angus had been on an all-day session and stopped in one of the bars for a drink. Apart from the German girls in there, his was the only white face. 'What the hell, it was so dark in there I didn't notice all those darkies,' he later said. He kept trying to chat up the girls. Eventually he went to the toilet and fell asleep. After ten minutes, the door was kicked in and he was hoisted off the pan by two black men. 'Fuck off, Sambo, I'm having a shit,' he shouted. They threw him into the street.

The next night, Angus waited at the station for his pals to arrive. As he stood there he was recognised by the Pompey 6.57 mob, so called because that was the time of the train they always left Portsmouth on when they travelled away. Normally the rivalries which happen in club football don't spill over into Europe, but this time one of the Pompey lads whacked Angus – he owed him one from a few seasons back. When Angus's pals turned up, it developed into a brief fight with a few punches thrown, causing the police to run over before all of them moved away mouthing threats at each other.

Later Angus, with his pals in tow, went back to the blacks' bar and sat on the same stool he had the night before. With him was Marcus, who was half-caste and had long dreadlocks. The German blacks, who all spoke with pseudo-American accents, asked Marcus what he was doing with white boys. 'These are my Chelsea pals,' he replied, which confused them even more. Nothing came of it, mostly because Angus couldn't remember any of the guys who'd thrown him into the street the previous evening.

Later that night, some of the lads tangled with a few pimps and other blacks. The Germans pulled out gas but Salford was faster on the draw and gassed them out before they could fire theirs. 'Our gas is better than yours, eh, Fritz?'

One German was down on the floor. Just as he was about to get paid out, another German pulled a gun. As soon as the word 'shooter' was heard, everybody got on their toes. No shots were fired.

To Salford, that was a defining moment. Hamburg was gas city. Lady canisters (lipstick-size, very handy, make a nice Xmas stocking filler for the wife), jumbo canisters, truncheons with gas. His eyes lit up when a friendly smiling Turk produced imitation firearms like magnums, which fired CS capsules. He was in heaven when he saw his favourite plaything – the exploding gas canister: 'Just right to set a whole bar moving.' 'Yeah Abdul, we're gonna gas out some Germans,' said Salford gleefully, rubbing his eyes and giving it the 'aargh' sound that people make when the gas hits them, the irony of which was not lost on the Turk.

By Tuesday, the firm numbered 60. The lads who had flown in via Pan Am had nicked the entire contents of the duty free shop and the carrier bags. We chinked as we jinked as we moved.

All the main faces were on board: Tony Cavelle, Giles, Skitsy Carl from Tooting, Steve Rolf, Pete Tate and Braddy Dave from Southampton (many years later Braddy was to end up in prison in the USA for drug running), Peg Leg and Damian Brown from Southend, Jock, Paul Gee and his pal Pete Vokes from Fulham as well as Gatwick Steve, Stuart Glass, John Bailey, a geezer called Bucket, and Paddington.

'Ou est le hauptbanhof, Fritz?' was Salford's favourite line for most of Tuesday morning, after he'd demolished a large amount of the stolen duty free. 'Multilingual and cunnilingual' was how Giles described him after his performance in the red light district the previous evening.

Our idea was to get a train from Hamburg on Tuesday, arriving in Copenhagen just after lunchtime on Wednesday. After the trouble with the Pompey lads nobody wanted to hang around the station, so the plan was to get to the station just before departure. That way, the police would also be caught unawares. Unfortunately, we cut it a little too fine and as we approached the barrier the train was pulling away. The quicker lads made it easily but I was struggling, running while carrying my bag. Unlike some who travel light I always like to dress well, so my bag was quite heavy. A scouse lad held the door open for me. 'Come on, mate, throw us your bag,' he shouted. Not on your life. I've seen that trick before. Throw 'em your bag and the door slams shut, leaving you with nothing, standing on a railway platform looking like a right mug. After all, they were scousers. The thought of them wearing my clothes gave me the impetus to catch the train. On the train they were all 'Well done, mate'. 'Yeah, lads, well done, indeed.' I smiled at them.

The train journey saw Salford consume the rest of the Pan Am duty free before passing out. Bad move, mate. By the time he alighted from the train, Salford was receiving some very funny looks – the other lads had borrowed lipstick from a lady passenger and had painted a red swastika on his forehead. It stayed there for hours.

We had arranged to meet everyone at the Spunk Bar, in the centre of Copenhagen. By the time our firm arrived, it was so crowded you couldn't move. While we were waiting outside, a beer lorry pulled up to make a delivery. The driver and his mate went across the road for their dinner break. If they had printed invitations stating 'please thieve from our lorry' they couldn't have done any better. Within minutes, half the lorry was being unloaded and carried up the road. People inside the bar left their drinks and came outside to help themselves.

In the centre of Copenhagen is the Carlsberg Brewery. Every day it has guided tours and at the end of the tour you are invited to sample the beer and to enjoy the Danish hospitality. As fast as you drink it, they provide you with more: 'You like our Danish beer?' Of course we did, but free methylated spirits would have been consumed by that mob. A one-legged York fan got so pissed that when the fresh air hit him he fell flat on his face and his false leg fell off, leaving him lying in the gutter, literally legless. Everybody fell about laughing, with nobody helping him up. The Danes going about their work and shopping looked on and smiled, as Danes do.

Outside the ground, some scousers were selling tickets, doing their best imitation of needing to work to earn money. They were certainly getting plenty of scowls. Touting is okay, but taking money from travelling England fans is frowned upon. Near the ground was a sentry box, and inside was the archetypal friendly Dane selling tickets. Salford kicked in the side, while someone else grabbed fistfuls of tickets. Salford got his foot stuck and was shouting for help. Sod that. Everyone thought it was just another wind-up and shot off down the road. 'Don't leave me, lads,' he howled. Everybody half-expected him to pull his foot out, shout 'April fool', then run off. The last we saw of him he was under arrest. Around the corner, we put the scousers out of business. Tickets for sale became tickets for free to England fans, leaving the scousers out of pocket.

Inside the ground, there were no plain-clothes policemen offering a stand-up fight, but row after row of riot police. This time all the fans were put straight back onto their trains after the match, Salford excepted – he had an extended holiday in Denmark when he received two months for robbery at a special after-match court. When he returned he told us that the Danish prison was cleaner than his London flat, which wasn't surprising when you saw the food stains on his clothes. By all accounts, it was the best he had eaten in years. He looked almost healthy, a frightening thought.

Paul Scarrott was 32 and at the height of his drinking and fighting abilities. The year 1988 was the finest hour for some, and the few were vilified by the many pressmen out to capture the battles in every minute detail. Euro '88 was being held in Germany, and for two months Scarrott had been telling anybody who would listen about how England would be renewing its acquaintance with Rommel. Manfred Rommel, none other than the son of Field Marshal Rommel, the Desert Fox, was the mayor of Stuttgart and the English hooligan army would be descending upon his city. Manfred, like all Germans, held out a hand of friendship and waited to welcome us. Scarrott, like many other fans, didn't understand this mentality. He never did make it to Stuttgart – the Ministry nicknamed Scarrott Public Enemy Number One and the German authorities arrested him after street disturbances in Dusseldorf and deported him. What was in reality a brief skirmish between German and English youths became blown up into the 'Battle of Dusseldorf Railway Station' with Scarrott leading the English charge. It conjured up images of Richard the Lionheart and General Montgomery. It was the stuff that legends are made of.

There was a lot of talk of travelling out to Spain for the international in February 1987. February is a crap month for football unless you are challenging for the League title, and there wasn't much chance of that with Chelsea at the time, so a trip to Spain by coach would be fun. By the time we left the Hand and Flower pub on 15 February, the coach was full of fans from different teams tagging along, just for a laugh. Altogether, 66 were on board. Chelsea were the largest group on the coach with Stuart Glass, Darren Crewe, Andy Rutledge, Dell Boy from Battersea, Mickey Smith and Darlington. There were also Scarrott and Gary from Nottingham, a couple of Pompey lads, Craig Allison from Aston Villa, some Palace chaps, Chris and two Shrewsbury lads, Peter Vokes and Paul Grover from Fulham.

As the coach pulled away, a huge cheer went up. Next stop Paris, we hoped. First, though, we had to get through customs at Dover. The coach driver was paranoid about getting tugged by the police for having alcohol on board, so he asked us not to drink between London and Dover.

One of the lads had made some calling cards up and had them translated into Spanish: 'Congratulations, you have met the Chelsea Headhunters, No 1 in England.' We saw that as a nice touch. Everybody wanted one of those.

The tone of the journey was set by Giles Denslow. It was a typically horrible February day with an east wind driving the sleet into your face, making you scrunch up your eyes to keep it out, and that damp type of cold which gets right into your bones. Travelling to Spain for the football, it was enough to make you think about emigrating to the sunshine permanently. Unperturbed by this, Giles Denslow turned up for the trip in shorts, a huge sombrero, an Ibiza T-shirt and those Clark's-style summer sandals with no socks.

'Wearing socks is very uncool and typically English,' he informed us. As if to make himself immune to the cold, he stood outside for a few minutes while we remained inside and shivered for him.

As if it was an eccentrics' convention, Eddie Mills arrived with a giant Paddington Bear-style suitcase. Since that day he has been known as Suitcase Eddie. Salford was dressed in his usual trampish manner in his regulation donkey jacket, DM boots and jeans that had a life of their own. Alongside him was his regular

England travelling companion, the Manchester City Bin Man, Dave Blezzard.

Salford was an uneasy travelling companion because he was so intense about his political beliefs and was unpredictable – although he made most people laugh, others were nervous around him. He was good fun and humorous but you had to accept the package as a whole. His claim to infamy was of one of his pilgrimages to watch Glasgow Rangers, this time in Dublin, which added an extra edge to the match. During the journey between Holyhead and Dublin, Salford achieved his usual state of complete intoxication. This resulted in him punching a priest as they disembarked. In the mayhem that ensued, an Irish garda hit him in the face with a truncheon, blinding him in one eye. Whilst this prevented him from being charged with a very serious offence (punching a priest in Ireland would have copped him a long prison term had he not lost an eye), it meant that he now looked at people with a slightly sideways glance, making even those who knew him a little nervous as it gave him the look of a madman.

Fellow traveller, that complete madman Paul Scarrott, turned up complete with false one-year passport in the name of Al Capone. (Scarrott definitely started a fashion. During Euro '98 guys named Freddie Krueger, Frank Sinatra and Robert de Niro were thrown out of Germany.) Making the clickety-click noises of the Prince Buster tune, he informed us noisily that Al Capone's enemies don't argue. 'What is this, a bleedin' madmen's convention?' shouted one of the lads from the back of the coach.

We arrived without incident in Paris early the next morning. The coach parked just underneath the Eiffel Tower. It was crisp and clear, very cold, with white wispy snowflakes blowing around. Giles looked up at the tower: 'Where are we, Blackpool?' he exclaimed. By now he had decided that the Spanish uniform would have to give way to something more sensible, so Suitcase Eddie was relieved of some of his warm clothing while he was asleep.

Small groups headed off in different directions, with

instructions to be back at an agreed meeting time. Giles tagged along with a group of 20 lads heading for the Latin Quarter. For some reason, they thought that meant they were going to bump into groups of Italians looking for it. What they did bump into in the early morning as they walked along the banks of the River Seine were two African street cleaners. 'I wonder if it's true that blacks can't swim,' someone said, so without further ado they chucked both of them straight into the water. The water was icy cold and it was incredible that they didn't die of shock. After a few seconds they struggled out on to the bank. 'No,' said Giles, 'it's a fallacy, they can swim after all.' 'Paris is full of black immigrants, the rest are middle class,' is a quote I remember.

The Latin Quarter was all art shops, poncey stuff, so after a cursory glance the lads caught the Metro a few stops into the Pigalle. What else is there to do in Paris except for finding an English pub and settle down for a serious drink? Why else would you come to Paris, except to drink in the Rose and Crown? After all, Paris is a city that does tours of its sewers.

After an hour or so, Giles got bored and got a small crew together for a river cruise. Everywhere they looked, people were pissing into the Seine – and to think that the French look down on the English. As they cruised up the Seine, a boatload of Japanese tourists came the other way. 'Get a load of this, Nippon,' Giles shouted and dropped his trousers to flash his bum at them. One of the Japanese shouted and then the whole lot of them raced over to snap it, making us think that the boat was about to keel over. The sound of the camera shutters whirring, along with the funny squeal Japanese tourists make when they see something unusual, was quite incredible.

As they disembarked, Giles did his party piece and ran out with the contents of the boat's till. Seconds later a Vietnamese guy came rushing out. Everybody sprinted for it and ended up in a restaurant laughing and joking. A couple of minutes later the boat owner's face appeared at the window. 'You very handsome man, my wife love you long, long time,' shouted Giles in a mock-Vietnamese accent. With that, the guy held a gun at the window.

'I shoot you. You are a very bad man,' he shouted.

'Sod that, he's got a gun,' shouted someone. With that everyone was off, through the kitchen and out the back alley, never stopping to look back. Everybody was waiting for the sound of a gunshot and the pain in the back but it never came.

As evening fell, the lads became the focus for the groups of Africans and Arabs who were hanging around and were getting heaps of abuse, most of it because they didn't drink. 'You can't be a real man if you don't drink, can you?' was the considered reasoning. Being able to hold your drink as well as fight was what being English was all about. What started the trouble, though, wasn't the level of abuse, but the fact that someone touched up one of their girls as she walked past. All hell broke loose, but Salford was well armed with his gas canisters, and this as well as a barrage of bottles put them to flight. Yet everywhere we looked they were there lurking in the shadows, waiting for one of us to venture somewhere we shouldn't.

As we retreated into the bar, a large police presence turned up and a number of them came in. One of them saw a gas canister on top of the table. He picked it up, shouted something in French then squirted himself in the face with the gas. It took a few seconds, then he ran out of the bar. He obviously told his colleagues what had happened because they didn't attack us. Instead, the head of the police wanted us back at our coach and they piled us into vans. As we drove away, we suddenly realised the enormity of the problem we had created – there must have been half of African/Arabic Paris waiting for us in the sidestreets.

Back at the coach, we caught up on the gossip. One of Scarrott's Nottingham mates, who was very quiet on the coach journey down, had been arrested. He had been sitting in a bar when he was insulted in French by a waiter when he demanded a beer: 'S'il vous plait est un langage international, Anglais.' He didn't understand exactly what was said but didn't like the tone so he jumped up onto the table. 'This is what I think of your country,' he shouted, then dropped his trousers and deposited a steamy one on the table. For a few seconds the whole bar was stunned. He jumped down and sprained his ankle, which is how he got himself caught and arrested.

He should have known better than to travel with Scarrott. This was a man who seemed to have a habit of getting fellow travellers arrested. On a trip to Switzerland, Bin Man tagged along with him. En route, they got off the train in Austria for a beer. As they were sitting in the bar they saw some locals depositing money in a wall safe. Scarrott slipped out, went into a hotel and took the fire axe, then went across the road and tried to axe the safe off the wall. Bin Man, sitting in the bar faceless drunk, copped a three-month stretch for his part, despite telling the Austrian magistrate that he'd only known Scarrott for a few hours.

The police watched us leave Paris, minus the six of us who were being held for 'theft, assault and associated offences', as they put it. The coach sped south with none of us giving a second thought to those who had been arrested. It was an occupational hazard. Most people slept. At the Hendaye/Irun border crossing, the coach pulled into a service station. Inside, one guy was serving. While one of our party went into the restaurant to eat a meal, the rest helped themselves, practically looting the shop.

Back on the coach Scarrott had 50 reels of film but no camera. He had reasoned that somebody would have brought a camera, but he was out of luck. Also on the coach were a large number of sombreros, as well as liqueurs covering every colour you could possibly imagine, plus some you couldn't. Scarrott and Salford were tasting them all.

The further south we went, the worse the weather became. As we pulled into Burgos it was snowing heavily. Thirty of us went into the old town, a fort, for a drink. We ended up in a bar full of medieval armour and artefacts. Giles got hold of a crossbow. The owner came rushing across and had one of those Spanish-English conversations.

'No, no,' he went. 'Pow, whoosh malo.' He intimated that it

worked and could kill someone. With that, Giles picked up the crossbow and pretended to fire it. Accidentally, the catch went and the bolt inside was fired off. It shot past those at the bar and thudded into a suit of armour. The owner went spare, grabbing the crossbow and shouting: 'Loco Anglaisy, loco Anglaisy.'

'Just what is his problem?' retorted Giles.

Once again we had attracted the ire of the locals and a scuffle started outside the bar. Meanwhile a fight had broken out at the disco in the town, and a local Spaniard had pulled a knife. One of the Chelsea lads saw him do it and hit him with a chair. In the ensuing mêlée two of the locals ended up getting stabbed, and the Chelsea lads got a pasting. Back they came to the bar we were in. Once inside, fighting broke out again. This time, though, Salford let off a gas canister after we had all gone outside, then we held the doors closed. The people inside were up against the glass coughing and spluttering, trying to get out. Then we let go of the doors and made a run for it. They staggered out onto the street and fell onto the pavement, holding their stomachs and eyes, staggering around, vomiting, the full works.

The next morning, the police arrived at the coach and arrested everyone. The senior police officer made a solemn announcement: 'We are going to have an identity parade and hold for trial those identified.' One by one we filed past the police and the two witnesses, who were sporting marks to the face. One of the chaps who had been in the thick of it pulled his hood up and put a scarf over his face. Unbelievably, he was allowed to pass. Paul Grover, however, was immediately spotted. Perhaps it was his poor complexion which made him stand out. That was the end of the Fulham Two, as Peter Vokes had been arrested in San Sebastian for looting a Burberry and Lacoste shop.

Paul Grover received a six-week sentence. He was one unlucky chap, because in Marseilles in 1998 he was the only one of six English people jailed after the trouble between the English and the local Tunisians. The witnesses picked out another four who, despite protesting their innocence loudly, were driven off at speed with the car's blue lights flashing.

The snow was getting heavy now and it lent the Spanish landscape a surreal quality. Not that it bothered Scarrott, who was wearing his sombrero and singing 'Si Si Señora' for the umpteenth time.

A few hours later we entered Madrid. The cold air was reflected in the faces of the Spaniards, who looked discomfited by it. It was obvious that this weather was a shock to them. They were well wrapped-up but somehow it didn't look quite right, as if they were more used to bright, summer clothing. Salford was contemptuous of the architecture and the people in general, shouting derogatory comments about their heritage.

The coach pulled up outside the magnificent Bernabau Stadium in Madrid. It was an impressive sight as it seemed to tower almost into the clouds, but that didn't bother Salford, who immediately led a raid on the stand outside, looting it of T-shirts and badges, most of which had been thrown away by the time we reached the first bar.

Eventually, we set up camp in a small bar two stops down on the underground, and had San Miguels all round. As we prepared to leave, Salford stood up on a table: 'Right, you lot. This is Spain and they are all filthy Catholics here. Remember that the Pope is the anti-Christ and that you must never, ever trust a Spaniard. If it wasn't for Drake defeating the Armada, we would be a colony of these morons. We burned their boats off Cadiz and now it is time for us to show these heathens once more that we are all good English Protestants. We'll go out of here and roar straight into the first mob of dagos that we find. Is that understood?' He had a manic look in his eyes. For those who didn't know him, listening to him must have been a sobering experience. Everyone nodded, although there were some perplexed looks amongst us. 'Is he for real?' someone whispered.

We left the bar. Coming out of the restaurant opposite at the same time was Terry Venables, now managing Barcelona and here for the match. 'Behave yourselves, lads,' he chirped in a bouncy voice, as if he was our best cockney mate.

'Fuck off, you yid,' shouted Salford in a reference to him

having left Chelsea to play for Spurs. Terry hurried away, shocked at the reception he had received from his fellow countrymen.

Further down the road were a group of Spaniards. Salford roared into them, letting them have it with both barrels of his gas cartridges. They scattered but then regrouped and it became a running battle all the way to the ground. At least it kept us warm.

When we had finally arrived at the ground it was 18 February and we'd been travelling since the evening of the 15th. We had lost a few souls along the way, but this was what we were here for – to support our country. We were welcomed by unsmiling police as we went through the entrance. Inside the ground, the cold started to come up through our shoes, into our feet. We were positioned on a terrace behind the goal, with Spaniards spitting at us from above. At half-time, what someone thought was rain was in fact piss coming through the concrete above our heads. I experienced the worst feeling in the world as falling piss went down the back of my neck in the gap between my scarf and hair, sending a horrible cold shiver down the length of my spine. The knowledge of what caused the feeling made it even worse.

England played well and won the match 4–2, but the cold made this seem like an afterthought. As we left the ground there was a huge mob of Spaniards, at least 2,000 strong, waiting for us. You're scared at moments like these, but you know your mates won't lose it, and you hold it together because that's the way it has to be. Two thousand against 60 don't look like good odds on paper but, surprisingly, the numbers in this sort of scenario are irrelevant if every one of your firm decides to have a go. The Spaniards started advancing, but we started chanting and in the dark corners the sound echoed and reverberated, making it sound as though there were thousands of us. 'We're the north stand, We're the north stand, We're the north stand Stamford Bridge.'

'Come on, let's do it, let's fucking do 'em,' someone frantically shouted in the midst of the grunting, roaring and shuffling sounds a large crowd makes exiting a ground. Then, the most vile blood-curdling roar from the depths of hell was uttered by Salford and a few others and the entire group charged. The

Spaniards had already been backing off from the noise of our chanting, but the charge made them scatter. Small irregular fist-fights broke out. Dell Boy from Battersea saw one Spaniard with a brick advancing towards him. He was just about to pitch it when Derek lurched forward and caught him flush on the jaw. His lights went straight out, and he went down still holding his brick. Dell Boy picked it up and launched it into the retreating mob of his mates, causing one of them to go down. None of the Spaniards waited to help their mates, but legged it while the two on the ground copped a kicking. This was no poseurs' battle, waiting for the police to arrive and save you – it was every man for himself, a fight for survival and the Spaniards knew it. They backed right off, shocked at our ferocity, then waited at a safe distance for any single stragglers to leave our group.

Eventually the police arrived and we returned to the coach in high spirits, only to be greeted by the sight of smashed windows. The thought of the cold journey chilled everyone, but there was nothing we could do. Just as we were about to leave, some West Ham boys came up and asked if they could get on our coach. 'Clear off, you've been sneering at us for years. Now piss off and take your chances elsewhere. You think you're so bloody hard. Now go and prove it,' shouted Dell Boy at them. When it suited them, they wanted to be all English together, but any other time they'd be whacking out our guys. Well, now they had their just rewards. They slinked off – good riddance.

We left Madrid huddled together for warmth, advancing slowly up the motorway in the worst blizzard Spain had seen in 40 years.

The coach crawled north along the E25, with visibility of no more than a few yards. We passed the sign for Aranda de Duerro and after that the terrain became even more mountainous. The blizzard seemed to worsen. The Spanish landscape just didn't look right covered in snow. We felt like Buzz Aldrin looking across the Sea of Tranquillity for the first time. The snow reflected an eerie light.

I was sitting at the front and, like most people, I fell asleep.

Suddenly, I was awoken by the most almighty crash, and found myself flung out of my seat. There was a horrible grinding of metal and smashing of glass, and after what seemed like an eternity, the coach shuddered to a halt. Shouts and groans filled the air. All the lights were out in the coach, but there was a faint glow from the snow. I looked around. The coach had hit a lorry which was parked up in the right-hand lane and had skidded to a halt. No lights were visible on the lorry.

By now, people were staggering out of the coach covered in cuts and bruises. The only explanation for the crash was that the driver of the lorry must have fallen asleep at the wheel. He climbed down. 'There he is, get the bastard!' someone shouted. With that, the driver ran across the road to the other side and sprinted away across the fields.

The scene was one of utter devastation. Then there came a sound I never want to hear again as long as I live – out of the darkness came a lorry. The driver saw us, hit his brakes and pressed his horn. The sound of that lorry braking and skidding out of control made me feel sick to the pit of my stomach. I thought for a moment it was going to take us out like ninepins, but the driver regained control and continued on his way, not even bothering to stop. With that, somebody rushed forward and got a torch from our coach driver then ran down the road waving it frantically. We heard the sound of lorries honking as they saw the torchlight being shone. Whoever did that deserved a George Medal. They were risking their life, especially as the Spanish lorry drivers were speeding like maniacs in the dangerous conditions.

Then came the terrible realisation that one of our mates was trapped in the wreckage. All we could see was a pair of trainers, not moving.

'That's Andy's red Adidas,' said a voice in the darkness. It was Andy Rutledge who was trapped in the mangled wreckage of the coach. Looking at the state of it, I couldn't believe how many of us had got out without any damage.

'Andy, Andy, can you hear us?' Nothing, not a sound, not even moaning.

'Pull him out,' shouted someone. So everybody tried to pull him free, but he was firmly trapped – pull as we might, he didn't move.

'Stop pulling, we might damage him further if he's not already dead,' I shouted. Still they tried. 'No!' I yelled at them until they stopped. We stood there waiting in the freezing cold.

Eventually, the emergency services turned up. At least we now had a red light further down the road to stop any lorries crashing into us. They got out, looked at the coach, had a discussion in animated Spanish and stood there.

'Do something, then, you dago wanker,' shouted Dell Boy. One of them intimated that he had no cutting gear, while his mate got on the radio. By now every emergency vehicle in Burgos must have turned up. The cutting gear finally arrived and Andy was cut out and placed gingerly in an ambulance. He looked close to death. The ambulance sped off while we were put into vans and bussed into Burgos.

When we arrived we were met by the mayor: 'Welcome to Burgos. I am so sorry that you are coming to my wonderful town in such circumstances, but we will put you up in the Hotel Fernan Gonzalez where you can have free accommodation, food and drink and telephone calls back to your families in England. Those of you who require medical attention will be taken to hospital and returned here after treatment, or kept in if necessary.'

Scarrot was moaning about his arm and went off in an ambulance. What a sight he looked in his stupid sombrero, by now crumpled and smelling of piss. He was right proud of the fact that his sombrero had prevented piss from landing on him. '*Touché*, dirty dago,' he had shouted up at the Spaniards while others swore and cursed as the piss fell on them.

An hour later, he was brought back to the hotel by two very stern-faced policemen. As he walked in, he winked at me: 'I've got just the thing to do the machines with.' I had no idea what he was talking about. He told us what had happened. While he was in the hospital waiting-room, he had slipped out, smashed a window and stolen a magnum of champagne then started drinking it. He had got halfway through when he was called for treatment, so he stuffed it down his trousers and walked awkwardly in. Thinking he had damaged his leg, the staff tried to get his trousers off and realised he had a bottle stuffed down there. They then told the police to throw him out.

During the journey back to the hotel, he spotted a tool kit in the back of the car and stuffed that up his jumper. All he seemed worried about was the fact that the police had confiscated his unfinished champagne. 'There's Schubert and now Scarrott with an unfinished one,' I said to him. Scarrott looked perplexed then told everyone how he was going to do all the machines in the hotel as he now had 'the equipment'.

Within ten minutes, the two policemen were back at the hotel spitting blood. The manager got us all into the lobby and translated the policeman's stern words: unless the emergency tool kit was returned, everybody was going to be kicked out of the hotel. Without further ado and as calm as you like, Scarrott produced it, walked forward and placed it at the feet of the two policemen. They looked at him in complete incredulity. You could see it in their eyes: 'What sort of person are you?' They barked something in Spanish at the hotel manager, then walked away with a shake of their heads.

I don't know what sort of bush telegraph they have in Burgos, but within a short while a hostile crowd had started gathering outside the hotel. That precluded any of us from revisiting the disco we had earlier gassed out. Someone even had the daft idea of going to see the lads who were in jail because of our previous visit a couple of days ago.

The next morning, while everybody congregated in the breakfast room, the *Sun* informed England what we had been up to: 'GARY SCORES 4 AS YOBS SHAME ENGLAND; 500 GO ON RAMPAGE.' In the same report, it stated that four England fans had been stabbed before the match. Ted Croker, the FA secretary, was devastated. Not about the four stabbed fans – no, he was devastated about the violence caused by English fans.

Suddenly, as a few left the breakfast room a huge commotion broke out. People walked out to see what was going on.

'I don't believe it, he's given us a bill for £1,500 for food, accommodation and telephone calls.'

'Tell him to stuff it up his arse.'

It was all arm waving and remonstrating while we just shrugged our shoulders. A short time later a representative from the British Embassy, Vice-Consul Mike Murphy, turned up along with the mayor. He was ushered into a room and the door was shut. It looked like he was being held hostage until the money was paid either by us or him.

The £1,500 bill wasn't deterring us from ordering at will. The barman refused to open up a tab for Scarrott at the bar, so he obviously had some sense. Scarrott was ordering plenty of beer and persisted in calling every Spaniard Julio and Juan.

Some time later the British Embassy man, looking very white faced, came over and addressed us. 'You will be escorted by the police to Madrid via the train then taken to the British Embassy.'

Sure enough, we were soon on the train. As we pulled into Madrid, half the Spanish army was there to meet us. They directed us into buses with metal grilles over the windows. The way the locals looked at us was amazing. You would have thought we were Basque terrorists. I half-expected them to start pelting us with rotten vegetables. One old lady with more wrinkles on her face than an Ordnance Survey map and no front teeth stared at us. 'Do us a blow job,' shouted Scarrott.

We disembarked off the bus at the British Embassy only to be met by nobody and found the doors firmly shut. Someone pressed the buzzer. 'We are the England football fans who were involved in the coach crash. Please open the door.'

The answer that came back on the intercom stunned us: 'We are not letting you in. Go away.'

'Open the fucking door, you dago nonce.' Then silence. Someone pressed the buzzer again for about 20 seconds. 'Wanker!' he shouted down the intercom. He could have been shouting 'Mayday' into a force ten gale. Nobody was going to answer.

We stood there, stunned. After a few minutes we retreated to a bar and took stock. Then someone had an idea, and back we went to the door and buzzed again. 'Hello, my name is Alan Cartwright and I am a backpacker who has lost his passport. I need to see the British Consulate about getting a replacement.' All spoken in a very posh and correct English public school voice.

The buzzer sounded, opening the door and through we surged, past the startled security guard. 'Hello, Juan,' said Scarrott with a stupid grin as we flew past him. We then staged a sit-in, demanding to see the British Ambassador. There was nothing they could do about it as we were on British territory. When they threatened to evict us someone retorted, 'What are you gonna do, shoot us or watch us starve to death in Madrid?'

Eventually, someone came down to meet us. He looked very posh in his short-sleeved white shirt. Top of our list of demands was bacon rolls. They duly appeared about 30 minutes later. The man explained that as we had no insurance cover the British government was prepared to help us get back to England, but that we would be expected to pay the money back. He asked about those who had money and a few fools told him they did have some money, while everybody else kept quiet about whatever money they had in their pockets. The British Embassy representative then turned up and we gave him the bill.

A short while later a bus arrived to take us to the airport. It resembled one of Hickey's luxury coaches. 'Bloody hell, are we gonna be in another crash?' asked one guy.

Eventually we got to Madrid airport and traipsed over to the British Airways check-in desk. The man from the Embassy became involved in a long discussion with someone there. He walked away, saying 'Wait here.' He returned about ten minutes later. 'British Airways are refusing to have all 15 of you on board their plane.' A couple started shouting and swearing at him, while others shook their heads: 'Why?' He held his hands out. He seemed to know something more, but he wasn't saying. To give him credit, though, he asked us to stay put and then got ten of us onto an Iberia plane, but he couldn't get us all on.

The choice was another night in Madrid or a coach for the others. The five lads who chose the coach wished they hadn't. It took them three more days to get home. They arrived starving hungry and exhausted. For the lads on the Iberia plane, myself included, the wait on the tarmac seemed to go on forever.

As the plane took off we all let out a collective cheer, part happiness, part sigh of relief. As the plane climbed steeply, the landscape looked even more unforgiving. It was certainly a trip to remember, but for all the wrong reasons.

When we arrived back home, we were followed by hostile newspaper headlines from all over Europe, but we didn't care what they thought of us. Here are some examples:

France: The sickness of hooliganism comes from England like a scourge from the Middle Ages.
Great Britain: occupies the first place in Europe for its violence.
Italy: Barbarians live among us.
Germany: The English rowdies are no longer people – they are animals.
Spain: Some Britons cannot be controlled.
Belgium: Madness of hooligans. Keep the English out.

On Friday, 20 March, the *Sun* had its say:

NO MERCY FOR SOCCER YOBBOES IN BUS SMASH
A 'Thugs Special' coach waited in the snow for help for 80 minutes. No Spanish drivers stopped because they were too frightened. The travellers were reported to be skinheads and National Front. Andrew Rutledge, 18, was last night in hospital with head injuries in a critical condition.

Amazed Consul General Trevor Llewellyn came face to face with several fans, including one who was wearing an SAS style mask.

'It's not our fault. We were just passengers involved in a coach crash,' said Chris Henderson.

Then came the sickening part. While our friend lay in hospital fighting for his life, we endured the dubious distinction of being featured in 'The Sun Says' leader column:

> Do you wonder that the Spanish wouldn't help the English soccer hooligans lying injured in the snow after their coach crashed? The yobs had only gone to Spain to beat up the locals. Many of them carried visiting cards in English and Spanish . . . It would have served them right if they'd died in the snow.

You had to read that at least twice to take it in. Of all the excesses ever indulged in by the press, that had to be up there in the top ten worst.

Upon our arrival back in England, the *Sun* newspaper vultures were waiting. No sooner had the lads walked through customs control than the photographers were snapping away and stuffing microphones under everybody's noses. No one said anything, just gave them the withering looks of contempt which are all you're capable of when your body has gone beyond fatigue. One of the scribblers stated with real conviction, as if he believed it himself: 'Talk to us, we won't stitch you up . . . it's your chance to put the record straight.' Right, mate. Not that it made any difference, because by Monday they had another story and didn't bother printing anything more about us.

We heard through the grapevine that another tabloid paper had paid for the air ambulance to fly Andy home. He and all of the other 16 injured made a full recovery. It was a fitting tribute. In the world of the tabloids, we were leader-column material on Friday and a non-event by Monday. Not that we expected anything else. That summed it all up, really.

ONE SEASON OF INFAMY

FROM THE CASE NOTES OF 'OPERATION EXTRA TIME'
***REGINA V HENDERSON* AND OTHERS**

The allegations in this case concern the activities of a gang of so-called Chelsea FC supporters known as the Chelsea Firm or the Chelsea Headhunters.

The objective of the gang was to perpetrate acts of violence wherever possible either against rival football 'firms' or against innocent members of the public, in order to 'enhance' their own reputation as a 'hard' firm. On some occasions affrays would be planned to take place at the grounds of opposing football clubs, on others violence would occur if an opportunity presented itself on the way to or from away matches.

Although it is clear that the violence had been going on for a long time, the conspiracy period charged in this case is effectively the duration of the 1986–87 football season. The remaining charges are of substantive affrays. The defendants are variously charged where the evidence merits it. The evidence comes from a variety of sources, including from a small team of undercover officers (PCs McAree, Morrison and Sergeant Donnegan), and a team of 'spotters' headed by Sergeant Hobbs, nicknamed 'Flatcap' by various defendants. Much of the evidence goes to prove the conspiracy. Much of the violence planned was not successfully executed due to the intervention of the police.

━━━━━━━

We all read the case notes with interest. It was the first time I had heard of anybody calling PS Hobbs 'Flatcap'. Hobbs was a face at Chelsea in the same way as we were. He even knew our names and often addressed the known faces by their Christian names. The fact that the case notes stated that our violence was against innocent members of the public was absolute tosh. No innocent member of the public ever got attacked in 20 years of football violence.

━━━━━━━

On 4 March 1985, Chelsea played Sunderland in the semi-final of the old League Cup. Chelsea lost the away leg 2–0. For the home leg Chelsea played their hearts out, yet lost the match 3–2, with the one-time hero of the Shed, Clive 'Flasher' Walker, scoring twice. This was too much for some fans, who surged on to the pitch and were met by a wall of police and horses. One fan, John Leftley, tried to attack Clive Walker. In his everyday life he was an accountant. The *Daily Mail* said that as he ran towards Clive the crowd gave him a growl of approval. John never got to hit Clive, but his subsequent suspended sentence caused uproar from middle England, who expected civilised magistrates to exact revenge.

The same night Chelsea played Sunderland, West Ham were playing Wimbledon a few miles down the road. The crowd surged into Fulham Broadway underground station. On either side of the walkway were small shops with the shutters pulled firmly down. The police were trying to hold back the crowd from going down onto the platform where trains were pulling in with West Ham fans aboard. In the push and shove, a shout of 'You're nicked' went up and they saw a police officer roughly manhandling a poor fan. A loud shout went up of 'Rescue him! Rescue him!'. The crowd surged forward as one, and took back the fan, while the police officer was brushed aside.

All around the ground, the police lost control for a few mad minutes. You could see that struggling to maintain order and control wasn't an experience they enjoyed. The Chelsea lads knew that West Ham would have to take a train through Parsons Green to Earls Court. In the pitch darkness, the lads waited as the first empty train trundled past. Then a full one came along and stopped. It was full of claret and blue, and from it came the faint sound of the West Ham song, 'The Bells are Ringing for the Claret and Blue'. Across the tracks went Chelsea, armed with shovels, lumps of wood, scaffold poles, anything they could lay their hands on, including the entire contents of a BR workmen's shed. Everything they needed to lay waste to a train full of West Ham. By the time they had finished, the West Ham were shell shocked.

Two lads were sitting in the departure lounge bar.

'You Chelsea?'

'Depends – who's asking?'

By now, paranoia hung in the air like a 1950s London fog, all-engulfing and slow to disperse. The two lads looked shocked by our response to them, but everyone was now being ultra careful about who they spoke to. After all, his past conversations had a funny way of coming back to haunt Hickey. He'd never had any police officers on his coach, yet they'd managed to string out an 18-week trial on the back of overheard conversations.

The two lads were from Derby. 'We knew that Hickey,' said one.

'Yeah, great bloke,' added his mate.

'Really,' we replied. They were in full flow, with each of them telling us a different Hickey story, each outdoing the last, their supposed closeness to Hickey adding kudos to the fact that they were now travelling to watch England.

Who really gave a toss that they'd once met Hickey? They both wanted desperately to impress us with the fact that they knew a man who'd been famous for 15 minutes and had received ten years from the establishment. Then they started throwing in other names, smiling at each other as they reeled them off. It was pretty pathetic really, because Hickey had a small group of mates he travelled with and while outsiders were welcome to join his group, he never really embraced them. Funny that they were Derby fans – he hated the place after he got nicked up there, but the 'We knew Hickey and Ginger Terry' scene happened all the time. As we walked away, they smiled at each other.

Hickey called his coaches 'luxury coaches'. The only luxurious thing about them was getting off at the journey's end. Forever breaking down, the only thing to be said for them was that they were cheap. In the 1985–86 season, Stuart and I decided to go into the coach travel business. This time, it really would be a luxury coach. Roy Seaton laid on a double-decker coach with six TV screens throughout it. He even laid on a driver who was the spitting image of Rod Hull, which was good for a few laughs.

The stops were the Hand and Flower and the North London Tavern. No drink was allowed on the coach because we ran our own 'in-flight' bar service, with bottles of Stella Artois at £1 a go. Roy would travel over to France during the week on his OAP trips and get stocked up with beer. Another lad used to do regular trips to France as part of his work and this ensured a good supply of CS gas for the boys. He even had his sales patter: 'CS gas burns their eyes and it hurts,' he used to say as he took the cash and handed you the can.

The TV screens showed a regular fare of football-related violence from news clips which had been videoed and spliced together. There was also the 'Big Four' video, which someone had spliced together from porno movies and violence clips, making for hilarious viewing moments, watching Millwall smashing up Luton and then a couple in bed together.

If Stuart and I could fill a coach, we would clear £100 between us on a good day. If we didn't have enough bodies we used to drive the coach down to Euston and canvass for customers on the station concourse. It was good business.

Hickey had nicknamed us 'the young lot'. Now we were carving out a little niche for ourselves. We were creating a marketing ethos, selling the thrill of violence. 'Sod it, of course it will kick off on our coach.' There were people on the coach who weren't interested in rooting out the top boys in an arranged set to, just kicking it off.

Our 'bums on seats' strategy landed us with some right lunatics who couldn't tell you half the Chelsea players. They'd heard the marketing chat and wanted some of it. Football was the only place you could kick it off. They didn't give a toss about anything but joining the designer violence mob. They didn't even care if we lost the football match. For the first time, I heard someone start a chant in response to the away fans who were taunting Chelsea when they went 2–0 down: 'We hate football. We hate football.' Even the police looked shocked at that one.

Some of these guys just wanted to have a punch-up. Without punch-ups, you couldn't have filled the coach. 'Sure,' we used to tell them, 'we're gonna stop off on the way back for a fight.'

The aim of the guys on board who weren't obsessed with who their top boy was, or their main firm, was to terrorise home supporters. They didn't spend their time worrying, they just wanted to kick it off. Paul G from Fulham was one of the nutters we attracted. A diamond bloke, but a raving loony.

We went from the young lot to the designer violence mob in one fell swoop. For all their so-called undercover work, the police never travelled on the coach. The *Sunday People* launched a 'Shop a Yob' campaign. Nobody rang it. Here were the boys sitting on the coach covered head to foot in the most expensive designer clothes you could wish to see, some of them real pretty boys who spent hours grooming themselves, yet still they described us so: 'They leave litter everywhere. They relieve themselves with the same delicacy as a tom cat. They suck at cans of lager like the warthogs they resemble suck from a muddy pool.'

They must have been talking about someone else.

Chelsea were in Sheffield playing Sheffield Wednesday. Chelsea saw the Wednesday lads as dim-witted humourless Yorkies who were in awe of the Leeds boys, even if they professed to hate Leeds. They spent most of their time insulting the other Sheffield team, United, so our arrival was a good chance to insult the cockney style and ethos.

'You cockney wankers, we've got Yorkshire class,' one of them shouted once to Giles Denslow.

'I can see that. The style magazines are all up here, fighting and tripping over each other to see what you lot are doing and wearing,' he replied laconically.

Their whole end used to chant 'Yorkshire, Yorkshire, Yorkshire' in unison at us, like it was a great place to live, expecting us to chant 'London, London, London' back at them. We saw living in Yorkshire as a disease which could only be cured by moving further south. A small group of Leeds boys, not kids but middle-aged men, chanted 'Yorkshire, Yorkshire', part menace, part pride, at us from behind the protection of police lines. 'Okay, lads, now you've learned where you live you can set about learning some proper football chants.'

There had been a small scuffle near a housing estate and the Wednesday boys had scarpered. However, the local toughs and blacks living in the flats mobbed up and started throwing missiles at us. A few lads got on their toes.

Hickey disappeared and reappeared a few minutes later carrying two lumps of wood tied together in a cross. Leading the boys up the hill towards the Sheffield mob, he was singing 'Onward Christian Soldiers, Marching as to War'. Everyone filed in behind him and started marching and singing the song (substituting 'the cross of Chelsea' for 'Jesus'). At 20 paces, the Sheffield boys looked terrified at this group of 50 geezers laughing their heads off and singing, led by a religious fanatic. They ran away in sheer terror. A police van pulled up. 'What do you think you're doing with that wooden cross?'

'It's the Chelsea Christian Revivalist Movement, officer.'

Leeds were the team that the other teams on the eastern side of the Pennines measured themselves against. The way the Yorkies spoke about crossing the Pennines, you'd have thought they were a mountain range on a par with the Pyrennees or Alps, not a bunch of hills a couple of thousand feet high. On England trips, the northern lads would say that they had taken a liberty against the Leeds.

Leeds hated Manchester United more than anybody else, calling them scum with real vengeance and an edge in their voices, yet they always wanted to cut up against Chelsea. Nine times out of ten they were found wanting. They never came near our main pubs for a tear up, but Chelsea did their main boozer, The Black Lion, gave it a real going-over, smashing the windows with lumps of wood and pieces of concrete, then standing there beckoning them outside. 'Now that's what you call a service!' someone said as the lads moved on. The same pub was pinpointed by Alan Bladefold, known as Northern Al. Years later, he got life for murdering a black geezer in Chapeltown.

Leeds were always coming down to London in force and when they did, plenty of the lads would be out and about waiting for them. Like all northerners they loved the West End, walking around taking in the atmosphere, as they had nothing like it in their northern towns. One Saturday, Chelsea had a tidy firm waiting around in the West End with not a Leeds fan in sight. After a while, everybody decided to head back to Stamford Bridge for a drinking session. Unbelievably, the Leeds mob exited the Piccadilly Circus tube as we were entering. Without introduction, Chelsea tore into them. The Leeds boys must have thought it was a planned ambush. How could the Chelsea have known where they would appear? They scattered, leaving those upstairs to cop it. The ones who ran down the escalators were pursued with venom. The Leeds lads who ran down dead-end platforms didn't stop and bolted onto the tracks down into the darkness of the tunnels. The London Underground employees saw what was happening and immediately got on the telephone and had the power switched off. As everyone emerged back up the stairs, the whine of police sirens became a roar.

Later that day at the match, the Leeds lads smashed up the scoreboard. The police were thick on the ground outside. There was row after row of them, protecting the Leeds boys who looked like they'd had enough for the day. Into Fulham Broadway they went. Thinking that would be the last of it, everybody went for a drink, ending up in the Chelsea Drugstore. All the main faces were there, reminiscing.

Outside the Drugstore was a long line of camouflaged motor scooters. It was getting a lot of admiring glances from passing pedestrians. A few of the lads were standing outside while inside was a tidy firm of around 50 guys. Then a shout rang out: 'Have a look at this, boys!'

Walking up the road was a small firm of about 80 Leeds boys. Everybody waited inside for the mayhem to begin. They walked up and started kicking the scooters and were met by a tidal wave of people, glasses and other debris coming at them. Hickey attacked them with his famous Copenhagen kung fu kick. This time it was slightly more effective, as there were no Copenhagen riot police there to pay him out. Once again, Leeds scattered in abject terror. Our organisation was too much for them. I don't think they stopped running until they got to Sloane Square station.

Still they ranted on about how they were the hardest. When the leaflet campaign was at its peak, every firm had someone who must have sat up all night typing A4 and A5 leaflets, mostly on the old manual typewriters, complete with spelling and punctuation errors. Chelsea had Hickey sending out his silly one-liners guaranteed to make everybody shake their heads:

THIS MEANS YOU
CHELSEA MUST TAKE ASTON VILLA. EVERYONE MUST TURN UP.

CHELSEA FANS
MEET AT KING'S HEAD CHELSEA 11.30 A.M. FOR WEST HAM GAME.

DON'T MISS THE CHANCE TO TRAVEL BY HICKEY'S COACHES
   TO MAN. UTD ON 16 MAY.
IF YOU DON'T TURN UP ON THE 16TH YOUR MEMBERSHIP FOR
   NEXT SEASON ON HICKEY'S COACHES COULD BE AT RISK!!!!

This summed up Chelsea's attitude, really. Unlike Leeds, who won the award for the best-ever leaflet. Lenin would have been proud of this propaganda effort, shown here exactly as it was written:

LEEDS UNITED SERVICE CREW CHELSEA AWAY 9 OCT

These leaflets are for the loyal supporters of Leeds United FC. Not the christmas tress who sing Chelsea here we come in the safety of the Gelderd then do not show on the day. We are not ground wreckers, this sort of incident just attracts more pigs and other trouble i.e. FA inquiries which Leeds United do not want and cannot really afford. The service crew do not need a police escort. WE are the hardest in the land and have proved this everywhere. SCUM, YIDS, and even West ham have had to be honest and admit this. It was the service crew who stood at upton park and the market. NO other team in the land had done this at west ham. Scum ran all over the place. Yids are scared to go there, in fact all cockney cunts fear West Ham but LEEDS don't. We fear no one in England.

The service crew always stand together.

Today we will show chelsea what we think of them.

They reckon Leeds are easy. They are just mouth.

Fuck the Shed. Stamford Bridge is falling down. FUCK OF CHELSEA. WE met some of their boys down at Fulham last week. They did not want to know even though they outnumbered us, they ran like fuck.

And they will today. Leeds Utd service crew will stand together. Chelsea will bottle out on Feb 19th at ELLAND RD, SHELSEA DIE. NEWCASTKLE HERE WERE COME.

LEEDS UNITED FC pride of Yorkshire, pride of England.

DAVE LEEDS UNITED SERVICE CREW NATIONAL FRONT

The Leeds boys really showed us – well, they showed us their backs. Much to our amusement, the Leeds boys left stranded at Piccadilly Circus station cowering for their lives were picked up by the police and charged with threatening behaviour. The *News of the World* called it 'The Bloody Battle of Platform 4' and described them as: 'The notorious lunatic fringe who follow Leeds United.'

Chelsea, too, had their share of bad publicity, mainly to do with the National Front, but by the mid-'80s it had moved on. In 1980 the tabloid press had printed pictures of a Chelsea flag with the SS symbol sewn on, but those flags and pictures now appeared less and less. Leeds would graffiti the walls LUFC National Front, and some of the fans even wore Nazi armbands and regularly chanted 'Sieg Heil' in unison. As with fashion, Leeds fans took longer to move on than the rest of us did.

Later, they were involved in a riot in Birmingham which resulted in a judicial report from Lord Justice Poppelwell, who advocated banning all away fans. Eventually, some of the Leeds lads ended up the focus of an investigation. The Yorkshire police case was called 'Operation Wild Boar'.

At one time an east London accent meant exclusion from employment. Now, people from the home counties who follow Chelsea and other London teams cultivate a London burr in order to fit in. As proof that life has gone full circle, the flats once inhabited by the Brixton Bruisers in the '80s became desirable yuppie residencies with their monied residents becoming the flash new support at Chelsea.

West Ham considered themselves above this sort of thing, looking down on the home county poofs, who came into London for football. 'Most of your boys only come to Chelsea for a bit of inner-city street cred,' sneered an Arsenal boy at Chelsea one evening, after Hickey got nicked and everybody discovered that he hailed from Tunbridge Wells. This mentality was all-pervasive amongst the West Ham lot, who saw people from the sticks as less street-wise or tough than themselves. Something in their psyches made West Ham think they were special.

During his spell as an army officer, David Niven observed that the cockneys he met moaned about everything. It's true that cockneys are good moaners. From British Rail food to the litter left on railway platforms, which we threw, me and the boys could moan for England.

A true cockney must be born within the sound of Bow Bells, but so many West Ham fans claimed to be true cockneys that it beggared belief. Of course they were, just like each of the endless line of caravan fortune-tellers every year at the Epsom Derby is the only true Gypsy Rose Lee. Anyone east of Liverpool Street station is West Ham, as far as I'm concerned. That's where the streets start to get dirty, epitomised by the pub Dirty Dick's. For me, West Ham country really starts at Shoreditch church, just past the old Taces tool shop. Around the corner are the grim pubs in Temple Street. 'London Calling,' sang The Clash. The sound of litter and tin cans blowing in the wind. From here you carry on to Bethnal Green, and the trendy pubs where the West Ham boys stood outside, part of the ultimate pose. Only West Ham drank outside on the pavement parading their machismo, even in winter. Perhaps they had some Latino blood in them? Chelsea were flashy poofs, Spurs Yids, Millwall scumbags while Arsenal were runners.

Chelsea had long since learned that West Ham didn't just want a row, they wanted to humiliate you; to make you fearful of travelling past Dirty Dick's into real Indian country. Even the police down at West Ham had a strange sense of humour. Searching everybody trying to slip through the under-16s half-price entrance, then confiscating their cigarettes until the pile was 6ft high. Here you are, Sarge, a nice little smoke for you this week.

Arsenal and Wolves fans celebrated their Northbank, Liverpool their Kop with songs expressing the joy of being able to support their team from their terrace.

Not West Ham. Their Northbank reflected the fans' humourless demeanours. No music, just grey brick walls. Soon these lads moved into different areas first inhabiting the Chicken Run stand then moving into the far corner of the Southbank, boasting that nobody dared to come down to their manor; Upton Park and the Boleyn pub, full of Essex boys watching each other. 'I Always Feel Like Somebody's Watching Me' was on the jukebox for a while. Very apt. If it wasn't those irons, it was the Old Bill.

Even the tube train made you think twice about where you were travelling to. Meeting at Earls Court or Victoria, then on to the district line. The train trundles underneath the city of London then emerges into the light to be met by hundreds of industrial units stacked side by side – Lego meets ghetto. Hundreds of industrial units and Essex girls to go home to. 'What a fuckin' depressing thought!' shouted someone further down the carriage.

If Yorkshire was an acquired disease, Essex was a viral infection. Every inch of bare brick wall had been sprayed with the letters WHUFC and the crossed hammers logo. It was as hostile as the hammer and sickle painted on the walls of the Moscow Lubyanka.

Ford have obviously never heard of the Essex man mentality. They built a car factory and then watched their Essex men workers go on strike every other week. Then the Ministry told us about that friendly West Ham welcome and chirpy cockney humour: 'Fuck off home, you nonce.' Rough translation: 'Please retreat to the other side of the River Thames and take this punch in the face with you.'

Always, without fail, they had a welcoming committee waiting for you. It differed from the Millwall welcome in as much as they would sneer at every aspect of you, including your dress. Sometimes it was only two or three of them, but they always clocked you straight away, testing you with eye contact to see if your bottle was intact. You had to give it right back to them. Flinch an inch and they gave it to you big time. It was always eyeball to eyeball. You just had to hope the other fellow blinked first.

On 11 October 1986, Chelsea were determined to show those West Ham lads what was what. Giles Whitbread and I met at Camberwell Green and caught an early bus to Victoria station, which was its usual hubbub of frenetic activity, with buses pulling in and out between shoppers heading for the West End and the crowds descending into the London underground system. None of them gave us a second glance as we met Chris Walsh and Rob Cathrew.

Only last Easter, the police had boasted that all our generals and lieutenants were safely locked away and that Chelsea were finished. Now we had a tidy little firm of headcase Headhunters going down to West Ham for a livener.

We arranged to meet in the North London Tavern in Kilburn at around 11 or 12 o'clock, with the aim of travelling in a roundabout way to avoid the Old Bill and have it with their boys. Nobody telephoned each other. It was just a word of mouth meeting, and pretty soon around 150 to 200 of us were on parade. This wasn't to be an early-morning raid, just a show of strength from a determined mob.

Some went by tube, but our little firm decided to travel on the overground to Barking via a change at Gospel Oak, then change on to the tube. The train rattled along the district line with very little chatter amongst the lads going on. At each station we looked out onto the platforms, which were clear except for a few fans wearing West Ham scarves going the few stops down to Upton Park. One of them got in our carriage. Nobody took any notice of him. He was middle-aged and wearing a knitted woollen scarf, the type your granny used to knit at Christmas and that no self-respecting casual would be seen dead in, let alone wear to a match. 'Nice scarf,' said Giles, 'Mummy worried you'll catch a cold?' Everybody laughed and the West Ham fan looked nervous. He knew who we were. Deep down he knew we were no threat to him, but even so he was edgy. One day, a few seasons previously, I'd seen a couple of scarfers get off a train and someone hit one of them so hard that his two front teeth fell out, but that was the exception as I saw it.

The train rattled into Plaistow station around 2.20 p.m. and seemed to take an age to stop. As the doors opened a couple of the lads helped pull them apart manually, revealing that their nerves were on edge and that they needed things to move a little faster. 'Just like the '70s,' remarked Stuart.

We all alighted together, walking purposefully towards the exit. We handed our tickets in. The collector had a worried look in his eyes, pretending that he couldn't see the group as a collective, concentrating on collecting the tickets, pretending to look at the destination and dates on them as if he were checking and would pull us up if one were wrong. You could smell the fear on him, even though we weren't threatening him in any way.

We went out into the streets which looked similar to those anywhere else in London – a seemingly endless array of shops, almost every other one of them a fast-food outlet. Litter on the pavements and in the gutters, with the rubbish bins full to overflowing.

We were Chelsea and everybody knew it, except for the police van which pulled up alongside us then sped off, thinking we were West Ham. The weather was cold but the boys were designer-jacketed, with their hoods up or wearing baseball caps. We had around 60 to 90 boys out of the 150, the rest of whom everybody thought was in the pub. Some had slipped away elsewhere. Perhaps they had their own agendas or maybe the thought of taking on West Ham in their own back yard was too much for them.

It was a 15- to 20-minute walk to the ground and we'd have to go past plenty of their pubs, steamy-windowed from the hot breath of expectant football fans. Today none of those interested us except for one – The Boleyn.

Within seconds, a car pulled up alongside us. A nice friendly West Ham boy in his Ford Escort GTI. What else would their chaps be driving?

'It's part of their disease, it must be. "West Ham fan has

operation to have Ford Escort surgically removed from his arse",' said the person nearest the kerb.

'Nice to see you, boys. We thought you'd never get here. The lads are waiting for you around the corner.' Then he sped off.

'Says more about West Ham than a Mercedes ever can,' someone quipped. Everybody walked with a new sense of purpose, waiting to see if any West Ham were around and whether we could ambush them. Fifty yards down the road were a small group of young lads, under-fives, not faces from the main ICF firm. They watched waited until we were close enough for them to see that our dress code and demeanour meant that we were Chelsea. The advancing Chelsea lads broke into a half-canter then a run, but before the first trainer hit the pavement at a sprint the West Ham lads were on their toes, half-looking around as they sprinted for all their worth. We stopped running after a few paces. Some days people would be chased for miles, but today wouldn't be one of them. If West Ham wanted us they would find us. Suddenly, the Chelsea lads who had done most of the chasing came running back across the Barking Road. 'There's a right tidy firm coming towards us,' shouted one of them excitedly.

Around the corner they appeared, walking towards us slowly. This wasn't some bunch of idiots but their main firm – a tidy mob of about 200. No milk float today. Something inside told me they were tooled up to the eyeballs. The ICF face to face. Shit, this is the real thing, I thought.

Yuffy from Luton shouted out an idea: 'Spread out across the road, it will look like there are more of us.' A ridiculous thought; he might as well have shouted 'Circle the wagons', yet that is exactly what we did.

By now there were 60 at the front and around 30 sniffing the rear, as well as their rears, to see how it went. There were no police around, but there was no backing out now or it would mean a quick trip to casualty with a slash and a calling card left in the top pocket just for good measure. We recognised their faces. Some of them were nodding, indicating that this was the main event, arms slightly outstretched making the unmistakable beckoning motion with their fingers, some pointing out one person they wanted to settle a score with, while others walked forward with a half bounce, ready for the first contact.

One of our group fired a red flare which exploded on the ground, shooting red sparks in amazing patterns, right in the middle of them, causing a few to scatter and jump up and down, but most of them just kept on coming. Another flare fizzed through the air, this time at close range then it was off with fists and boots in the middle of the road. Nip and tuck, first with us getting them to back off and then them coming forward again.

Then it seemed like another mob was coming at us from nowhere. (Later someone said that they'd come from a pub in the housing estate.) Suddenly, someone was down and really copping it. Behind me a shout of 'Chelsea scum' and a knife sliced the air then through flesh. The shout of someone realising that the air slash had sliced human flesh, his flesh. A scream of anguish and terror. The horrible sound of pain filled the air and I turned around to see Jock drop to his knees, his face contorted, pulling his shoulders back. I ran over and kung fu kicked the man with the Stanley blade and he bounced back off the wall and retreated, coinciding with West Ham backing off across the road. The wail of sirens in the distance.

Another shout. 'Let's go at them. Come on.' That made the West Ham fans come back for one last little go, a grand finale before the blue curtain descended and spoiled the fun. But it ain't fun when it comes on top like this, in a really big dollop. Blows hitting you from every direction, your sides clenched in, waiting for the searing pain that comes a few seconds after the knifes slices you. Someone once told me that if you hold the two sides of a knife wound apart it doesn't hurt, because it is the touching nerve ends which cause pain. Thanks, you silly twit, as I finish bleeding to death at least I will have the consolation that it was painless.

'You Chelsea cunts, we're really gonna cut you up!' shouted one screaming fan, his face contorted by anger, spittle spraying with the venom of his words.

'Do 'em before Old Bill rescues them.'

Shouts filled the air. One Chelsea fan stood in the road and gave the shout, 'Who wants it then? Which one of you wankers is first?' West Ham didn't need a second invitation and forward they came.

I looked at the wound on Jock's back. It was a gaping slash wound, about ten inches long. Blood was pumping out of it and I held on to both sides to try and stop the bleeding. 'Bollocks, that was a new jumper,' shouted Jock, not realising the seriousness of what was going on around him and of his injury. I half dragged him back with another guy called Eric, as the West Ham boys came forward, raining blows on me and kicks into Jock's face and chest. I tried to back into a hairdresser's. Suddenly I felt a blow to my back. 'Stay out of here. Keep out,' I heard an effeminate voice said. I half-looked around and saw this permed poof, hair swept back with grey streaks showing through the Grecian 2000, hitting me with a mop.

'Let this guy in, he's bleeding to death.'

'Keep him out of my shop, then. Clear off, you thugs.' Great, my mate bleeding to death and him worried about getting blood on his lino.

For one second the mayhem stopped, then a group of three West Ham fans came towards us. I saw a knife in the hand of one of them and I looked at the face of the knifeman: 'Judgement day, Chubby.' Without warning, Chris Coffey from Kilburn came flying forward and jabbed the knife-carrying fan right in the chest with his best golf umbrella, causing him to stagger backwards and drop on to one knee with shock. Chris still had a broken nose from a fight with Newcastle a few weeks before, but it didn't stop him fighting like a madman. Chris really paid him out with a second violent stab right in the centre of his upper chest, puncturing the skin with the force of the blow. It shocked his two mates, and Chris went forward screaming and shouting, 'Come on, you cunts, we don't run,' whirling it around his head, hitting everything in his path.

Back they went, giving us a few seconds respite. A punch hit

Chris in the side of the head, then one on his already broken nose spread it right across his face and he bounced off a wall with blood squirting everywhere and gushing down over his top lip and chin. His eyes were blinking and he was in that area of half-consciousness where another blow would have completely scrambled his brain and put him out. He staggered around swinging the umbrella, trying to stay upright, fighting from instinct.

As the other West Ham lad came forward, the air was filled with a crack of an object making contact with a hard skull. The West Ham fan he'd struck was on his backside holding his head.

'Police officer, back off.' Armed with a small truncheon, the boy stood holding it up in the air, daring the lads to come forward. One lad tried, but he caught him. Chris sensed the mood, cleared his head and charged again alongside his new-found friend, who was a plain-clothes officer who thought it was time for him to blow his cover and come to the aid of poor Jock, who was completely white by now.

The sirens got louder, and flashing blue lights accompanied the screech of brakes. The nasty knife-wielder and his mates scattered, running, and disappeared before the police had a chance to grab them. Chris too was on his way, trying to find the rest of the firm, leaving me holding Jock's slash wound. The plain-clothes officer, who had saved Jock from a terrible beating, just flashed his badge, put away his truncheon and walked purposefully up the road.

'Do you want to accompany your friend to hospital?' asked the ambulanceman.

'No, I'll catch him later.' While the police were otherwise occupied, I slipped away with Eric and walked a few streets to rejoin the Chelsea lads.

The running battles had now spread to the adjoining streets, with police horses entering the fray. Overhead, the police helicopter whirred as it span in small circles, the blades cutting the air with a whipping sound. It felt like they were just above our heads, making you think you needed to duck. Blue lights flashing past, police everywhere – it's over for today.

Somebody had touched the twilight world of a near-death experience. It should have touched you, made you want to give it up, but you never felt those sentiments. People never said they couldn't take that sort of punishment any more, they either hacked it and got on with it, or disappeared. They knew their time had come and left the scene. Nobody ever heard the phrase, 'I'm getting too frightened'. Anyway, it wasn't fear in the true sense of the word. Not like the fear of warfare, when your destiny can be decided by someone miles away. No, your destiny would always be settled while you smelled their fear and yours intermingle.

Our aim was to get into the Northbank, the home of the West Ham fans, and run it. To show West Ham that they aren't the only ones who can take liberties in the opposing London end. The main entrance to the ground was policed by a few West Ham fans, but they weren't main faces, so we went on to the turnstiles. There were only 30 of us. Inside, a small group stood surveying the crowd. A chant went up from us: 'ICF ICF'. The idea was to make out to the police that we were West Ham, but those inside knew who we were.

'It's Chelsea,' came the shout. With that, the police barred our way to the turnstiles. 'Up the other end, boys.'

So to the South Bank. No sooner had we got inside the ground than a shout of 'ICF ICF' rang out, followed by the belching yellow of a smoke bomb going off. In came the West Ham, punching and kicking. While we had been at the other end, they had sneaked into the South Bank. The West Ham cut a swathe in the temporarily blinded Chelsea, but back we surged at them. All the West Ham main faces were standing there laughing their peculiar east London laugh, half-sneering half-gloating – told you not to mess with us. The police were in amongst us pushing us back, separating everybody. The West Ham crew got taken out.

Half-time, we were in the tea bar situated below the terrace.

Had they still been in our end the fight would have continued over a steaming hot cup of Bovril, chucked into someone's face to really get things going. It didn't matter how much you battered them, they'd still be there giving it plenty: 'Come on, Chelsea, we're in your end.'

Then outside in the famous undercover market area where they congregated, eyeing you up and laughing, both sides hurling abuse at each other.

Before the match, though, while their main boys ambushed us, Nashy and the Fulham boys had given the others what for outside the Queen's pub and in the market. Walking from Upton Park tube, they charged and ran the West Ham all the way to the ground, turning their sneers into panic. What a clique. There were only 30 to 40 of them, too. Nashy, Jointy and Matty dined out on that for a long time after.

After the match, police had it all worked out, keeping us in the ground for 15 minutes then escorting us back to the station. Right on cue, the West Ham stood outside their precious Queen's pub and shouted their threats, told us that they'd be up for some more later. 'You think that was a show, you wait till we see you later.' They'd see us on our turf. Big time, these boys.

We were at Victoria. Shake's Bar. Watching, waiting for the West Ham to come out. One hour – nothing. Our group of 60 or so moved on and sat in the Duke of York looking out of the windows, watching and waiting, our feelings of expectation heightened by the noise of footsteps on the wooden floorboards. The pub was split on two levels, but nobody went down to the second level. Outside was a police van and sitting in the front was Sergeant Hobbs, sticking out like a sore thumb. He wanted us to see him. 'Perhaps we should invite him in for a drink with us,' said one wag.

Every time a small group appeared on the bus station forecourt, everybody got up.

Eventually we were all so drunk we were beyond caring who turned up. The atmosphere changed, we became party-like. The Jam song 'Going Underground' came on the jukebox and people joined in. The police van revved its engine up and screeched off. London life had given them something else to do.

As 11 p.m. approached, we knew there would be no more for today. It was over. Perhaps the West Ham mob stood on Temple Street outside their new designer bars, resplendent in their short-sleeved shirts, drinking beer straight from the bottle while talking about how Chelsea matched them blow for blow. People drifted away, staggering across the forecourt, in danger of being hit by the buses swinging in. We'd missed the West Ham's game faces doing their cocky walk, swinging their arms around, moving their heads from side to side. 'Come on, Chelsea. It's your manor. Could you do this outside the Boleyn?' Would we want to was what we really wanted to ask them. As if we'd waste our time on a Saturday night going down somewhere as depressing as that. The lads don't go east to shag Essex birds. They are really terrifying. There would be no time for questions, though, if they did show. You're wasting your time talking to West Ham, unless it's a clenched fist. It is a 'Good evening, hammer, now wear this' type of conversation. This time, it was a number 36 bus ride home with only the previous night's graffiti for company.

———

Leicester away on a chilly November afternoon was always a difficult marketing proposition if you were trying to place 50 bums on seats. That morning, Stuart and I spent two hours at Euston trying to drum up enough custom to break even. The only way to do it was to promise the lads a day out.

Northampton is much like any other town in England. Any coach stopping in any town's centre on a Saturday evening would be guaranteed a welcoming reception from their finest locals, and we were no exception. For years, the Chelsea lads had terrified the Northampton fans, depending upon which team they followed. Now in the gloomy light of the Criterion pub, the locals looked at our small group warily. Pretty soon, they outnumbered the Chelsea lads by three to one. It always begins the same way, a slow move forward and then someone starts it, the brawl takes on a life of its own. 'Aargh,' screamed someone. The smell of gas was in the air, making people's eyes water. The pub was filled with the distinctive sound of table and chair legs cracking, followed by smashing glass as bodies hit the floor and rolled around. A bottle was thrown and it went through a window. That seemed to stop it all and everybody stood staring at each other. A couple of Chelsea lads had picked up the broken chair legs and were holding them. Outnumbered by three to one, we were backed up into a corner.

The landlord must have had a hotline to the nick because Old Bill were there in what seemed like seconds. 'Break it up, lads, settle down,' said the officer, as if he did this sort of thing every Saturday evening.

The locals had caught us unawares. Stuart had taken a bit of a whacking and he wasn't pleased. The head man of the Northampton posse was the object of his ire.

The stares and uneasy stand-off continued until closing time, when the police ushered us onto the coach.

'Bye-bye, Chelsea, better luck next time,' went one of their mouthy ones.

The coach went off, but that wasn't the end of it, because the local mob from the Criterion started mockingly waving goodbye.

'Turn this coach around,' shouted someone.

Paul G was up out of his seat: 'We've got a reputation to keep. We've got to show them that Chelsea Headhunters can't be pushed around.'

I thought that was funny as he was a fanatical Fulham fan. By now the shouts were coming up from everywhere.

'Stop the coach,' I told Roy. I was going to address everybody, but the moment it stopped Paul came past me at speed and the surge of people pushed me aside as they all charged off and went back down the street. I looked out. We were parked outside the Angel hotel.

They met the Criterion boys coming up at them in Bridge Street and had a toe-to-toe on equal terms. This time, the locals ran. The police turned up. They knew exactly who was to blame and arrested five of the group, including Stuart and Lee.

———————

Birmingham is called England's second capital city, but Chelsea fans have always given that honour to Manchester because the Mancs were so big on fashion and music. Manchester boys have a passion about them for football and life that the fans of the two biggest clubs of Birmingham, Aston Villa and Birmingham City, have never had. Villa away was always a good football day out and a chance to have a few drinks, because the Villa never bothered Chelsea.

Birmingham has always aroused strong emotions in people, for differing reasons. Salford hated Birmingham, not the fans so much as the town. He claimed it was because it was full of left-wing book shops. His ideal day out in Birmingham was to throw a Birmingham Celtic fan through one of those commie-loving shop windows. I don't think he ever got to live out that fantasy.

With the Villa match coming so soon after the Northampton business, I had no trouble selling out the coach as a revenge mission, with the added bonus that we would seek out some Birmingham fans in the city centre before the match.

We arrived, and coming to the end of yet another concrete walkway in the Bullring shopping centre, we saw a small mob. 'Brummie boys,' someone remarked. Then all hell broke loose. It seems that they had been looking for us and we for them. Adding to all this confusion, the police were on hand to ambush everybody. There was no time to think, we all just fragmented, scattering everywhere. As is always the case, people split into their immediate comfort groups, sticking together with those you knew you could reply upon. At times like this, arrest and incarceration are your biggest fears. You'd miss the match and the night out. You run on instinct, thinking on your feet. Sirens seemed to be just behind us, the noise echoing off the concrete jungle that is the Bullring. Great acoustics, I thought to myself.

'Get into a pub!' shouted Salford. Great idea. In we piled, beneath a sign depicting two dancing harlequins. Once inside The Jester's it was obvious what sort of bar it was – the pictures of muscled half-naked men adorning the walls gave it away, along with the looks from the all-male clientele.

'It's a faggots' palace,' snorted Salford in disgust. The sound system in there was pumping out some class soul music with a heavy hint of bass. The pub itself was inviting, so a few of the boys ordered up beers and stood around waiting. Salford was apoplectic, but everybody else thought it was a great wheeze. 'Calm down, Salford. Old Bill will never look for a group of Chelsea fans in a queers' pub.'

Like every well-organised excursion, the lads had all been issued with their rally point and the coach left Villa for the return match with the Northampton lads.

'No chance am I going back to Northampton,' said Roy Seaton firmly.

Despite our pleading, he wasn't having any of it.

Eventually he compromised on Dunstable, a satellite suburb of Luton. This time we went into the Saracen's Head and generally had a good time, playing pool. Then, near closing time, the inevitable stupid argument broke out, this time over a game of pool. One of the lads was hit across the head with a pool cue by some local half-wit. He hit him with the thick end so hard that it split the pool cue in half as well as cracking open the head of our travelling companion. Nobody needed an invitation to give the guy, plus a few of his mates, a sound beating. The fight spilled into the streets, where it became handbags at five paces. Eventually the police turned up and we went on our way, minus one of our group who was taken to hospital along with a couple of their guys. Roy thought it would be a calm journey back to London. 'We need to make a quick detour to Dunstable casualty department to get our mate,' someone said.

Like any large hospital on a Saturday night, the victims of pub fights littered the waiting-room like the walking wounded of a field-dressing station. As the drunken participants sober up, the reality of their pain and suffering fills the air with moans and groans. Around 15 of us marched across the green grass, slightly muddy underfoot, and entered briskly through the automatic doors, where we saw our opponents from a little while earlier. Other people turned to look at us, but we strode directly towards our friends. By now we could see the fear in their eyes. They knew what was coming. One of them got up to run, but he was knocked to the floor by a right-hander. He tried to crawl under chair but was being kicked. 'Stop that, you lot,' shouted a nurse sternly, as if that would have any effect, and then she turned and ran up the corridor shouting for help.

It was short and sweet. We took our friend back on the coach and dropped him off at a proper London casualty department just over an hour later. The ungrateful twit kept moaning about his head all the way back down the M1 motorway.

BORED IN THE DOCK

I HAVE DONE THE WALK FROM THE BRITANNIA to the White Hart on hundreds of occasions. Today was nothing special. Then, 'Chris', a voice called out. I turned around and saw a face I recognised. 'Hello, Sarge.'

'Chris, you're heading for a tumble. You are being watched and you're going to be arrested.' Then he walked away without turning back. What Hobbs said stopped me dead in my tracks. I kept walking towards the White Hart, then crossed the road against the flow of people coming out and into the covered walkway of Fulham Broadway tube.

I didn't even attend the match. I spent all weekend panicking. Was it a wind up? What was his reason?

First thing on Monday morning, I was in my solicitor's office in Camberwell. Nick Inge could see that I was flustered. In contrast, he was the sea of tranquillity. I blabbered at him. 'What shall I do, leave the country?'

'Chris, go about your business as usual. If you are going to be arrested then there's nothing you can do about it but wait. If it happens telephone me immediately and say nothing.'

I left his office none the wiser. Nick couldn't answer any of the questions that were swirling around in my head. Why would a police officer tell me what was going on? What was his motivation for doing so? Perhaps he wasn't happy about things at work.

Perhaps he'd got close to us and realised that we were not the savages of popular myth. I will never know the answer to those questions.

Somewhere along the line, our script of laughter and fun became a bad movie. Shit, we were Gloria Swanson in *Hollywood Boulevard*, sitting there thinking everybody saw us as glamorous, but it would be our bodies dead in the pool soon. We were no longer the stars, we were just extras on a wider screen and the scriptwriters were determined to write us all out.

Getting nicked is never a pleasant experience. Getting nicked at a Chelsea v Arsenal match because you've lost the hood to your coat is almost embarrassing. Arsenal didn't always bring a mob to Chelsea, but after their night-time ambush of Chelsea Highbury Fields, you just knew they would be coming to put on a show. 'Look at us, Chelsea, we can dish it out then turn up to gloat.'

Sure enough they appeared, too cocky for their own good. Chelsea were waiting and went at them, making them back off. In the scuffle I lost the hood to my Barbour-type jacket. I had paid a lot of money for the coat so I was peeved about losing the hood. I went back down and asked the policeman on the gate if I could go back in and look for it.

'You're Henderson, aren't you?' he asked

'Yes,' I replied, feeling quite smug that the police knew me by name. 'My name is Chris Henderson,' I went, mimicking the 'My name is Michael Caine' Madness song. My smugness lasted all of three seconds.

'We've been looking for you. You're under arrest.'

That was it. I looked at my watch. It was 3.10 p.m. on 7 March 1987. The match was ten minutes old. I had no idea what was about to happen. I wasn't to know it, but this would be my last Chelsea match at Stamford Bridge for some time. If I had known that, I'd have looked back and savoured the view. All I could think was that they could have nicked me before I paid to get in, saving me the entrance money. A ridiculous thought in retrospect. There was no dawn raid for me in front of hundreds of TV cameras. As I was escorted away, I looked around in vain for the hood of my coat. The reality of what was happening wasn't sinking in.

At Fulham police station, other fans were in, mainly on charges of threatening words and behaviour. I sat there hoping to get my hood back from a kindly officer, but the words 'You're Henderson' when they arrested me started to spook me, once I got over the loss of that insignificant piece of clothing.

As I sat there, my thoughts turned to Hickey, Terry and all those who had passed this way before me. Getting arrested for fighting at football was part of the turf, but this was different. I began to sense that I might be here for some time. I felt weak inside, but I knew that I couldn't show any fear or weakness. I had to make them show their hand then prove whatever they were going to throw at me. They called me up to the desk and read the charge out to me. They claimed that I had incited a crowd to beat up an inspector who had been at the match, and that I had thrown a punch at him, shouting 'I've waited for this, you cunt'. Later in a written statement, Police Inspector Thompson said that he had arrested me lawfully in the police station.

They left me for a while in a cell, and then I heard the sound of the door being unlocked. One uniformed officer stood there. I tried to look impassive, but my heart was beating faster. Play the game, I thought to myself.

'We want to do an interview.'

'Not without my solicitor.'

'Really.'

'Yeah, I want my solicitor so give me my free call.'

It was a Saturday, so they were surprised that I would have access to a solicitor's number. They were looking at me with expressions that said, 'Come on, don't waste our time, make your confession and save us all a lot of hassle.'

The officer slammed the door shut, went away and returned ten minutes later: 'Come with me.' They sat me down. 'What's the number?' I wrote it out and they dialled, then he handed me the telephone. I explained the situation and Nick Inge arrived very quickly. The police were somewhat surprised about how organised I seemed.

We walked down a corridor into a small room. In the middle was a table, one chair on my side and two on theirs side. One of them had to go and get another chair, which really pissed him off. Two CID officers started asking me questions. They claimed to be undercover officers who had been watching me for some time at football matches, but I didn't recognise them. Funny that, I thought, any one of us could recognise a member of another football firm at 50 paces as well as an off-duty police officer, yet this cunning pair had managed to fool me. I was about to say that, but kept quiet.

Also with the main interviewer was a man with a moustache. I detected a hint of a geordie accent. They tried all the tricks.

'Your friends have already grassed you up. It's best you come clean.'

'Nothing to say.'

'You'll go down for a long time if you keep quiet.'

I shrugged.

'What does that mean?' geordie asked, imitating my shrug and allowing a hint of aggression to creep in.

I shrugged again. I could see I was getting to them.

Then they gave their hand away, making me realise that they were looking at a far bigger picture – I wasn't in here for assaulting an inspector.

'You're down as the ringleader in a conspiracy.'

I just shrugged.

I think they realised then that they had given the game away. My arrest was the catalyst for a wave of further arrests which happened over a period of time and which the police named 'Operation Extra Time'.

Shortly after that they left and I had a brief conference with my solicitor. I told him that my strategy was to say nothing and told him it would be best for him to be around if and when they charged me, and he agreed. When he left, I felt envious that he could walk out of the door and I couldn't. The police then asked for my consent to search my house. I gave it – if I hadn't, they would only have got a warrant.

Shortly after Nick left, they came in and told me they wanted to do a strip search. I think it was part of a softening-up process. I stripped off and they left me there naked, thinking it would embarrass me. 'Listen, lads, I've been all around the country dropping my trousers, so standing here in the buff is no problem.' While I stood there, I amused myself thinking about the Chelsea fan from Victoria, Noel Carroll, who had dropped his trousers to moon at a group of Sunderland fans, and had been arrested then jailed for seven days for insulting behaviour by an unsmiling woman magistrate. They soon gave me back my clothes.

The next two days settled into a routine. The police would tell me they wanted to interview me, then fire questions at me. I would tell them I had nothing to say. They would leave looking more aggrieved every time.

———

In they walked again, the business crew. They had already tried the smiling routine. Now they came through the door with speed and aggression.

'You are down as the organiser of the offs. Affray is serious. The maximum sentence is life,' went the first one.

'It's serious, this affray,' added his mate.

The other one leaned over. I could smell the food he had eaten earlier, definitely a fry-up in the canteen. 'We know it's highly organised. Everyone else is putting you down as the main face.'

The questions were being fired at me at machine-gun speed. I wouldn't have been able to answer them even if I had wanted to.

After five minutes of this, they asked me what I wanted to say.

'If you know so much, you might as well throw in the Brinks Mat job while you're at it.'

That was enough. They went out at the same speed they came in at.

Late on the second day, they came in and issued their worst threat yet. It nearly made me crack.

'If you don't say anything, we're going to go out and nick every Chelsea face, bring them in here and tell them that you're grassing everybody up. What do you say about that?'

Nothing to say.

After that, they got so angry they tried torture. They put me in a shared cell with two incoherently drunk winos, and they really stank. The police must have gone out especially to get them to put in my cell. Drifting into half-sleep, I kept waking up to these two babbling fools mumbling in their sleep. Then they woke me up with that horrible spitting and coughing, the TB type of cough. Half their lungs came up and they spat them out. Halfway through the night, I heard the sound of water trickling onto the floor as one of them pissed himself while he slept, just lying in it as if this was nothing unusual. By the morning it had dried on him, but the disgusting smell of dried piss followed him as he got up and walked around. A small puddle lay on the floor next to where he was sleeping. The mattresses were thin foam covered in plastic, but wear and tear meant that the foam was exposed. That smell would pervade it, giving a nasty smell for the next person who slept on it. When they came to release him, he smiled at me and walked out.

That next morning, Tweedledee and Tweedledum looked very pleased with themselves.

'Good night's rest, Henderson?'

I laughed at them: 'Stinking winos. Bring on another load tonight. Being a dustman in London, I'm used to that sort of smell and shit. I've seen maggots as big as a small cigar and rats as big as cats, mate. You should be more worried about which high-class restaurants I've seen them coming out of.' They never tried the wino trick again.

What followed was a game of cat and mouse. I refused to answer any of their questions. 'Nothing to say' became my catchphrase. It became a routine, and the gaps between interviews extended, giving me more time to admire the graffiti on the walls and enjoy the food repeating on me. The longer it went on, the stronger I got. They had thrown their best shot with the grassing trick.

Being on the chubby side, I loved my food. On the first day I ate the usual police station food: fried everything with a plastic knife and fork. Fried eggs over-easy and bacon with all the grease for breakfast. Fried whatever with chips for lunch, then a gastronomic fish fry-up in the evening. How's your heart, Sarge? Mugs of insipid-tasting tea, as if there was a law stopping them from letting it brew too long. Because I hadn't been charged, I was allowed food in the cell. By the second day my girlfriend was bringing me in Kentucky Fried Chicken and Chinese takeaways.

On the third day, the two officers came in and produced a Stanley knife.

'We took this from a toolbox we found in your house.'

I looked at them and burst out laughing. Then they produced three calling cards. I don't know where they got them from, but it certainly wasn't from my house. They were not particularly well printed. On them were written in blurry lettering on a white background: 'You can hate as long as you fear, for we are the Chelsea Headhunters' and 'Congratulations, you have been nominated and dealt with by the Chelsea loyalists.'

'Do you recognise these cards?' one of them asked me.

'Never seen them before in my life,' I replied.

Then they produced their *pièce de resistance*. The calling card written in Spanish. They'd had it translated, so they knew what it said.

'What does this say, Mr Henderson?'

'It's the name of the Spanish hotel I stayed in.'

At the end of the fourth day of questioning a senior officer came into my cell.

'Are you going to say anything at all?'

'No. Nothing to say.'

'That's what I thought. We are not going to waste our time any further asking you questions. We are going to apply to have you remanded in custody.' I looked at him, and at the officer behind him. They were looking for a reaction. I showed none. The police hate that, they want you to break down, to beg for bail; then perhaps they can get you to talk, in return for them putting in a good word for you. Anybody who has experience of the system knows that that is all TV bollocks.

The police, as good as their word, opposed bail on the grounds that I'd be likely to commit further offences. I was remanded to Brixton and then transferred to Wormwood Scrubs. After I had been on remand for a month, the lads started appearing and telling me they too had been charged.

On remand, we met fans from other teams, such as the Millwall two, along with West Ham and QPR fans, at Wormwood Scrubs. It's funny: on the outside we were enemies, yet on the inside we laughed and joked about everything, giving each other banter when any of our teams lost, something which would have caused a major confrontation on the outside. Perhaps it would have been different if we'd been remanded at a prison in their manor, considering the way West Ham used to put it about at England matches when they had the superior numbers.

One day some Cambridge lads were transferred in. These were part of a gang who were responsible for attacking a group of innocent Chelsea scarfers outside a pub. The cowards, claiming to be part of the main Cambridge firm, viciously cut the throat of a poor travelling fan named David Ayling in revenge for a slight from Chelsea the previous year, instead of having it out with the real Chelsea faces.

As one of the QPR lads knew a screw, we arranged for a note to be put under their cell doors late at night. The idea was to terrify them. Unfortunately, the note, reading 'You are going to die – Chelsea Headhunters', went under the wrong door and the next day a huge rastafarian confronted us in the exercise yard.

'Which one of you ras clats (rough translation is 'bloody tampax') is going to kill me?' We looked at each other, unsure of what he was talking about until he produced the note. When we explained what had happened, the rastafarian was eager to be part of such an honourable enterprise and took it upon himself to personally terrorise the Cambridge fans. We couldn't have planned it better if we'd tried.

The game went on for the next 65 days, until I was granted bail on 11 May 1987. Once the football season was finished, they could hardly argue that I was likely to commit further offences. Mind you, the conditions were pretty stringent. My passport was retained by the police, which meant Butlin's instead of Ibiza for my summer holiday. I had to remain resident at my home address and I was banned from attending any Chelsea football match, either in the close season or next season. I also had to report to Camberwell police station at 3 p.m. every Saturday afternoon.

Eleven months later, on 11 April 1988, our criminal trial started. Sitting in Knightsbridge Crown Court we faced a jury of 12 of our peers. This time the police, unlike at Hickey's trial, were not going to have it all their own way. We knew that they were going to try and bring in anti-Semitic remarks and other anti-social behaviour, to make out that we were part of some far right conspiracy.

We had worked hard to get a jury who might understand our behaviour, white and working-class preferably. We didn't want any blacks on the jury because of our right-wing past. Despite black Willie's presence at Hickey's trial, the prosecution still accused the group of being National Front. Working-class people, preferably around our age group, who'd had previous dealings with the police would be best.

Every one of the accused could reject three potential jurors. The first thing we asked everybody to do was swear their oath on the New Testament – that would preclude any Jews, who used to swear on the Old Testament. We knew the Spurs chant of 'Yiddo' would be brought up, even though none of us would know a Jew if we saw one, much less discriminate against one.

On the first day, both sides were rejecting anyone who didn't represent their ideal person. In the afternoon the court ran out of potential jurors, such were the number of objections. Eventually, 12 good people and true were found and sworn in. Hickey and the boys never bothered with this part so our having done it gave us a glow of confidence.

The only part of the trial that was initally in the police's favour was the startling statement made by Anthony Cullen. We hardly knew him, but he must have sat in the interview room and had the delusion that he was a fiction writer. Some of the things he said were astounding, attributing this and that to everybody. It's one thing knowing you haven't done what you've been charged with, and quite another being fitted up like that. That's enough to make even the hardest of the hard nervous. Stanley Alley, Newcastle and West Ham at their worst paled into insignificance by comparison. At the back of everyone's minds were the harsh sentences that had been dished out to Kevin Whitton, Hickey, Ginger Terry and the rest.

The press were waiting in the wings to hang, draw and quarter us.

Two days before the hearing, Cullen disappeared. In true King's Cross rumour mode, we all knew that he'd done a bunk to Ireland. The police knew that one of the main planks of their case, somebody who was supposed to have been there and apparently had seen us do it, was gone. They were outside the court.

'Where's Cullen, then, Plod?' one of Stuart's mates in a mocking tone asked a group of police officers waiting outside the court. Stuart had not been arrested until 6 May, and then it was mostly because of the tales of violence that 'Roald Dahl' Cullen, the storyteller *par excellence*, had told the police. They must have loved it when he started writing. I bet the only problem they had was keeping up with the amount of paper he must have used up.

'Yeah, where's your fucking top boy now? Out to grass?' added another. The police pretended not to hear. The boys could have been next to a fence, mocking another firm for not turning up at Chelsea. The lads said they felt good afterwards. If they'd said that outside Stamford Bridge they would have been nicked for threatening behaviour, but here in the court the police had to take it on the chin.

Before the start of the trial, our bail conditions were explained to us. We had to be downstairs in the court every morning 20 minutes before the proceedings started. The police would then take us all up together by the back stairs. In the evening they kept us behind to prevent us from bumping into any members of the jury.

Every day we had to surrender our bail, then go into the custody of the court and wait in a little room. Then we waited. Some people had newspapers, but most of us found it difficult to concentrate in the early days, so we sat there making football fan small talk: who Chelsea had signed, our thoughts on the future, the forthcoming European Championships in Germany and Scarrott's determination to take it to the land of the hun. It reminded us of the interminable waits we all endured over the years, following Chelsea. Waiting is something all football fans become accustomed to. Sometimes we would have a chat with our respective legal teams, or else the barristers would get involved in legal arguments upstairs before the court started, so we would often have a little time before we were called. We could have been at King's Cross waiting for a train, or sitting in the coach heading north up the M1. The stories and the laughter flowed.

In the press, Operation Extra Time was portrayed as the culmination of another painstaking undercover operation by policemen infiltrating our ranks. We were seen as a threat to the fabric of society, and to the existence of football culture itself.

Alongside me in the dock as a fellow conspirator was my best mate, Stuart Anthony Glass. We'd been skinheads together before we became weekend coach entrepreneurs. In real life, if there was such a thing for football fans, he was a removals man and lived in Hounslow. Contrary to popular opinion, though, football violence wasn't real life; to us, it was a substitute for cheap video rentals. Jeremy Allen Bodkin was also on trial. He was another south London lad who, unbeknownst to us, had kept a diary. Just like Terry Last, it would come back to haunt him. The others were Giles Alan Whitbread from the Isle of Dogs, who worked as a brickie: the same profile as that of many hooligans conforming to the one printed by the Ministry. Loads of money, liked to work hard, drink hard, spend fast and have a bit of argy-bargie. Lee Elmer from Hemel Hempstead, council worker. Michael Smith from Colliers Wood, a great bloke and an absolutely mad Chelsea fan. He had a fight on his wedding night with a Spurs fan and was the type who would wear Chelsea underpants and be proud to tell you so.

Mark Howard Baldwin was there too – just a coach passenger who paid his money and came along. Hard as it was for those who'd been brought up on a diet of organised violence with generals and foot soldiers, there were people who just turned up each week, paid their money and enjoyed a day out. Sometimes they played cards, other times they sat buried in a book. Mark was one of these types. Quite what he was doing here was beyond Stuart, Giles and myself. The wrong place at the wrong time. He was no angel, but that could describe thousands of other young men who enjoyed a drink and went to football. There were people who only went along for a punch-up, and you had to sell the thrill of that sometimes to make a profit. (We called it the constructive marketing of our unique sales proposition.) Mark wasn't one of those guys, though.

The list was long. Martin Huggins: a coach passenger, nicknamed Linky because he looked like the Missing Link. Martin was a staunch loyalist and was into the Rangers thing and all that William of Orange stuff. Also charged were Gary Duckett and Trevor Reed. Those two never came on our coach, and although we knew them, we were surprised that they had been charged as part of our conspiracy. They'd been involved in a fracas with Arsenal at the match on 7 March 1987, so perhaps they had been lumped in, but they had never hung around with our mob – they ran with the Wandsworth crew.

During the questioning the prosecution came up with a number of incidents – Parsons Green affray of 4 March 1985;

High Street, Kensington of 12 October 1985; West Ham United on 11 October 1986, which also included a fight on the Barking Road; a fight in Northampton and Dunstable which the police classed as an affray. Finally, there was the trouble between us and Arsenal. During the months preceding the trial, I'd had numerous conversations with my legal team. Every news report on the TV about football violence weakened our case. The popular misconception was that we were going out and kicking the shit out of old ladies and throwing babies out of prams. My barrister didn't know how the jury would perceive us, so he found it difficult to weigh up our chances of a successful defence, although none of us had any intentions of holding our hands up and pleading guilty. No surrender, Mr Plod. We had to stick together, pretend that the courtroom was really a windy street in some hick town and the prosecution was another firm, the 'us against them' mentality. If we stuck together, at least we had a chance. My lawyer told me that I needed a not guilty verdict. Otherwise I was looking at around seven years.

Heading up the prosecution team was Brian Lett, who had also been the prosecutor in Hickey's case. I remembered some of the derogatory comments Hickey had made about Brian Lett, but to me he was just another opponent. He had his job to do. I never really took much notice of him. This was his manor.

The demarcation lines were on show in exactly the same way they were in the world we inhabited. Their trademark, 'Good morning, ladies and gentlemen of the jury', could have been any one of us introducing ourselves to a rival firm. The more we noticed it, the more striking the similarities became. I wondered what teams they all supported, and tried to guess from their characteristics and mannerisms. For the most part all of us were indifferent. Immediately Trevor Reed and Gary Duckett were eliminated from our case as their offence was an isolated incident at a single match. We waved them a cheery goodbye as they departed while they wished us luck. The words of Geoffrey Boycott going into bat, 'It's not luck, it's skill', rang true. For the first few days the case was outlined in the court, then they got straight into it. The jury elected a male foreman. He looked like he knew his way around the terraces. On the third day, the foreman came in wearing a West Ham top. Stuart and I looked at each other, exchanging smiles and the 'Yes' look fans give each other when their team is awarded a penalty, a look that says, 'The ball isn't in the net yet but it's as near as damn it.'

The police had obtained the video we used to show on the coaches which someone had culled together from TV footage. On it were hundreds of clips of violence, and the jury sat through the whole four hours. However, right in the middle was a comedy sketch featuring Gryff Rhys Jones and Mel Smith, set in a courtroom in which they were prosecuting football fans, using chants. The judge watched stony-faced for a few minutes, then burst out laughing at the humour of it all along with the jury, the court staff and everybody else. The laughter exposed the folly of the prosecution's claim that we had used the tape to whip everyone up into a state of frenzied violence. Only the prosecution team failed to see the funny side of it. The jury had a sense of humour, but they didn't.

One evening we left the court and caught the tube. By coincidence, in the same carriage as us were two of the female jurors. We exchanged glances and smiles, but nothing was said.

Considering the stakes we were being tried for, we should have taken more interest in the proceedings than we did. I had seen what they did to Hickey in the witness box and decided not to go through the same thing. They had no incriminating statements from me, and I had said nothing in the four days at the police station. The worst they could throw at me was to link the fact that I was once a public schoolboy, having attended Seaford College in Petworth, Sussex, to the pasts of Hickey and Ginger Terry. I could see the press having a field day with that one. The prosecution tried to make me out to be some sort of general, but the fact that I had admitted to nothing was on my side.

Part of our modus operandi as Chelsea fans were the 'ooh ooh ooh' sounds we used to make when advancing on other fans. This tactic was very effective. The police must have briefed their legal team and explained how it was used to rout opposing mobs. PC MacAree was in the dock answering questions. Lett asked him about the grunting. Lett's voice took on a more solemn tone as he tried to explain how terrifying it was, and how the concerted use of it caused mass panic. In a crowd confrontation situation, when 50 to 100 people are doing it, it is very effective, but explaining this to a well-ordered courtroom was proving difficult for the prosecution. I looked over at the judge, who was frowning as he tried to understand. He asked for a further explanation. Brian Lett explained to the court how it worked: 'Ladies and gentlemen of the jury, the Chelsea Headhunters used to exacerbate their violence by uttering a low, rhythmic grunting sound as they advanced towards opposing fans, before attacking them. This was in the form of an "ooh" sound.' Lett tried to give the 'ooh' a working-class accent, but his clipped voice couldn't make it work.

The judge looked over at Brian Lett and held his finger up to indicate an interruption. 'I am unsure of what you mean. Perhaps PC McAree could do it for the court's benefit.'

McAree looked at the judge questioningly, doubting the seriousness of the request. When a mob of Chelsea fans are doing it walking towards the opposition it sounded fearsome, but in the sterile silence of Knightsbridge Crown Court it was ridiculous.

'Go ahead, PC McAree,' the judge said, moving his fingers to encourage commencement.

'Ooh ooh,' he went, then looked at the judge, whose expression indicated that he didn't yet fully comprehend. McAree added a final flourish, trying to add a bit more brevity to the sound, but he sounded like a gorilla with bronchitis. 'Ooh ooh ooh ooh ooh,' he said in a slightly camp voice, causing the lads in the dock to start laughing. The laughter spread to the jury, especially the young foreman. A couple of them put their hands over their eyes because they didn't want to be seen laughing so much.

'Hmm,' the judge mused. 'Is that it?' He looked to me as if he thought the line of questioning invited ridicule.

'Yes,' answered PC McAree.

The judge looked over at us, sitting there in fits of giggles, as if to say that he couldn't see how that sound terrorised the general public.

'Thank you for that. Please continue, Mr Lett.'

When Lett sat down, my barrister Charles Salmon stood up smiling. 'No questions,' he said, and I could swear he added an extra elevation to the end of the 'no' so that it sounded ever so slightly like 'noo'. Maybe it was his way of mocking the prosecution.

During the trial, we were under the jursdiction of the court from Monday to Friday. We received new bail on the condition that we signed on at the police station every Saturday, and continued to stay away from any Chelsea matches, even though the season was drawing to a close.

Sometimes I would drift away as if the whole trial wasn't happening, staring into space on another interminable coach journey in my mind, with the motorway flashing past in a blur, time standing still, unable to remember what I was focusing on before I drifted away. Then I would look up and someone would be speaking in a dreary monotone, explaining this and that for the benefit of the jury. That was my abiding memory. Nobody lost it in court. No, that was frowned upon, because doing so would signify weakness. Everybody had to be seen to be in control. It was in marked contrast to the football matches, where losing it is all part of the experience. That is why some of the prosecution's graphic descriptions of our supposed mayhem must have been hard to swallow. Try and explain to someone in an MFI showroom the majesty and beauty of the Mona Lisa. You couldn't do it.

On the afternoon of Tuesday 22 March, a female juror fell ill. The judge advisedly decided to adjourn the court for 24 hours to give her time to recover. He informed us that we had to report back to the court on Thursday morning, and would still be held under its jurisdiction. We couldn't believe our luck. On the Wednesday evening, England were playing Holland at Wembley. The game had been depicted in the press as the hooligan grudge match of all time. As it turned out, thousands of English fans met at Baker Street, and stopped all the traffic, while no Dutch showed.

Earlier in the day, some Derby fans took advantage of their superior numbers to slap some Chelsea fans about in Leicester Square.

Myself, Stuart, Micky Smith and Martin Higgins travelled to Baker Street, where we met the full Chelsea firm of 150 to 200 Chelsea lads. We travelled back to Leicester Square around 4 p.m. to set the Derby lads straight. Unbelievably, we caught 20 of them face on at the top of the escalators. There was no small chat. This was slap on sight. They scattered everywhere, pushing startled commuters to the ground in their rush to escape. The majority of the group leapt back across the barriers to street level, while four or five ran down the escalators towards the tube. Stuart and I hurtled down the metal steps after them.

Coming up the opposite way were three police officers in uniform. As we came down, two of them stood looking at us, open-mouthed. They were the same officers involved in our case.

'Henderson!' shouted one incredulously, unable to believe what he was seeing.

'Afternoon officers, nice to see you. Must dash – I have a train to catch.' I continued running.

We never caught up with the Derby fans, so returned to Baker Street where we ended up having a stand-off with the West Ham outside the Globe pub. Ridiculously, one of them informed us, 'We don't follow England, we're east London.'

'Oh, South African, are you?' I replied, referring to East London in South Africa. It was completely lost on him.

The next day at court, the police never said a word.

The case meandered on at a gentle pace. It entered its sixth week. How much longer could this tedium last before we all went back to normal life? Across London, the West Ham fans were also on trial on conspiracy charges. One evening, we went home to see Bill Gardner's ginger mop, Swallow and an assorted cast of belligerents on the TV news. 'Police case folds. West Ham fans walk free, acquitted on all charges.' It seemed that some discrepancies had been found in the police evidence.

The next day, Brian Lett addressed the court: 'You are

obviously aware of what has happened in another court regarding police evidence. Under the circumstances, the prosecution have decided to put the papers in this case forward for forensic scrutiny. The Crown are confident that this course of action will uphold the integrity of the evidence and that the case will be able to continue. The Crown are confident of being able to secure convictions.'

For a few days we all sweated, until we were called back into court on 18 May 1988. We sat downstairs in the room waiting to be called upstairs. Suddenly, we heard a refrain we all knew well, and had heard thousands of times before on the terraces. ''Ere we go. 'Ere we go. 'Ere we go.'

The tuneless a cappella melody from three or four chanting voices got louder and, along with the sound of fast footsteps, it echoed through the corridors. It was coming from our legal representatives. From the looks on their faces, I thought that they had won the pools and been offered a date with Miss World.

'It's all over, lads. The prosecution, after having the logs examined, have found discrepancies. They are going to offer no further evidence in this case.'

'So what does that mean?' asked Giles.

'You will go upstairs where the judge will inform the jury to formally acquit you.'

Free to go. It was music to our ears. Upstairs we went in a state of shock, shaking hands and slapping each other on the back.

In the court, a very humble Brian Lett told the court that he was unhappy about proceeding on the basis of the evidence, which appeared to have been tampered with. The forensic tests showed that eight of the 94 pages had been altered. The prosecution offered no more evidence. We were climbing the steps to collect our winners' medals.

The judge did his legal bit. As soon as the jury discharged their duty to acquit us, the judge awarded us costs and then turned to address us as a group.

'Gentlemen, you have so far behaved in an exemplary fashion. I understand that there are a large number of press outside waiting to speak with you and take photographs. I would very much appreciate it if you could leave the court with dignity.'

We all nodded at him and left the court. 'Cheers, mate,' went Stuart. The judge half smiled and acknowledged him. The prosecution looked shocked. Their post-mortem would have to wait for another day. We brushed past them, not even bothering to mock them as we would have done if we had been at a football match. From being the main firm, they were now down there with the dregs like Crystal Palace. No-hopers. What a shower.

Outside we were confronted by the press who snapped away, the whirring of their shutters sounding like a round of applause to our ears. The foreman of the jury was the first to congratulate us.

'Well done, lads, I thought you were innocent.'

Two of the female jurors came over and hugged us one by one.

We decided to go for a drink with some friends and well-wishers, who invited the two girls along. The press were desperate for a photo and we obliged outside a pub along with the three jurors.

The next day, the Ministry reacted with horror. Something had to be wrong. The football hooligans had been found not guilty. A more heinous crime was the fact that the jurors had spoken to us.

A tidal wave of criticism almost swamped the police. The press, who had spent years murdering us in print, turned on the police with venom, but then turned it onto the two female jurors and the male foreman for daring to come for a drink with us. This was supposed to undermine the whole jury system, something that baffled us, as the jury themselves had decided nothing.

The next day, we were supposed to have chanted 'Sieg heil' outside the court, and I was supposed to have told the press that the forthcoming European Championships in Germany would be a 'blitzkreig'. Nobody cared about the reality. Undercover surveillance and the reporting of it was like a Christmas pantomime now, the subject of untold ridicule, broken, a Humpty Dumpty of an operation that nothing could put back together.

Allan Green, the Director of Public Prosecutions, defended the role of the CPS in bringing the prosecutions. He claimed that: 'They could never have spotted the discrepancies in the police evidence . . . It was the authenticity rather than the content of the documents which came under scrutiny . . . The discrepancies to which you refer were not apparent to the naked eye and, in two of the three trials, were only revealed after many hours of detailed examination by forensic scientists.'

When the dust settled the police, like any good mob, came back for one more bite of the cherry. Jeremy Bodkin was rearrested and charged with two counts of affray. He had compiled a notebook entitled *Football Violence – What it is about, why it happens and who does it,* which he intended to be a full-scale documentation of the football hooligan's life. He had recorded in his diary details of the Kensington High Street and Parsons Green ambushes: 'Violence is like a drug. When you do something naughty and get away with it, it's exciting and you do it again. That's what it's like at football.' It came back to haunt him. In November 1988, Jeremy Bodkin was jailed for three years at Knightsbridge Crown Court for the Kensington High Street ambush.

OLD SOLDIERS

AFTER HIS LUCKY ESCAPE CHRIS HENDERSON 'RETIRED', moved to Thailand and opened a sports bar in Pattaya Beach, along with Hickey, who had his conviction quashed. Unwilling and seemingly unable to retire, some of the West Ham lads took it upon themselves to repeatedly telephone threats to the bar as they left their macho East London pubs, pathetic people who think there is still an on-going grudge ten years down the line.

Chris Henderson accepted £25,000 compensation from the British government to settle his malicious prosecution claim, almost six years after the jury acquitted him on conspiracy charges. Shortly after, his bar was visited by four men claiming to be West Ham fans on holiday, at 4 a.m., where they smashed up the bar and, extremely unusual for real West Ham fans, even smashed a picture of West Ham's favourite son, Bobby Moore, holding the World Cup aloft. The Thai girl serving behind the bar remarked that they had short, well-groomed hair, as if they were in the forces!

There was one last calling card to end them all:

ICF
We done Millwall
At The Den 3 Dec '88
IRONS KILL LIONS
22 April '89

You had to pinch yourself to believe that a human being had actually written that. Chelsea had been involved in more newspaper column inches than any other group of fans, although never for celebrating the death of another football fan.

As the last football hooligan trial was abandoned by the government, it looked as if it really was all over, but everything that goes around comes around. It was December 1990, an all-ticket Chelsea v. Spurs match. All was quiet in the Ifield Tavern in Cathcart Road when the Spurs boys made their move, putting in the windows. Spurs boys at Chelsea, looking for it – it really was a crazy mixed-up world. Out it spilled on to the street, with pool cues and stakes made from saplings. Scotland Yard stated that they were investigating the affray: 'Iron bars, wooden poles and bottles were all used. Between 150 and 200 football fans were involved. The rear bar of the pub was wrecked, a 12ft by 12ft plate window, valued at £2,500, was smashed, together with two windows in neighbouring houses, and seven motor vehicles in a street nearby, valued at £3,500, were damaged. We have no reports of injuries but we found stakes and iron bars with blood on them.'

As their middle-aged spread means that everybody is auditioning for bit parts in the Brixton Bruisers firm, the old adversaries mostly laugh together over a beer or three. Not always though. The once infamous Queen's pub in West Ham was visited by a mob of Manc Reds, complete with lumps of wood and balaclavas covering their faces. The bemused Essex-man West Ham drinkers in there took their whacking on the chin, unable to comprehend the fact that they were now paying the price of the excesses of their retired predecessors. At England games, some of the northern lads still go looking for it with the London boys, who just want to let sleeping dogs lie and enjoy their retirement.

Mostly though, the old malice is dead between the 40-somethings who exchanged insults and blows across the English landscape. The usual recourse for the old faces is to relive past confrontations over a chilled lager, laughing about their ridiculous exploits. One thing everyone has in common, though, is that they only remember the times when they were in the ascendancy. The times they were humiliated at some obscure railway junction are, as always, conveniently forgotten.

For some, though, the enmity will never go away, and the playground games continue. Those that cannot graduate from the hooligan's academy must suffer the ignominious stares of an incredulous public, who cannot believe that a 50-year-old man still marches down the road looking for an off. Meanwhile, in Holland, the Feyenoord and Ajax gangs organise an early-morning set-piece battle on the edge of a motorway, co-ordinating with their mobile telephones the exact point of contact, leaving several seriously injured and one dead man at the side of the road.

'The end is nigh' brigade at Wembley gradually dwindled away. For 30 years they had watched our seasons of mayhem in the walk along Olympic Way with their doom-laden exhortations. It looked like perhaps they had been right after all when the announcement came that Wembley Stadium was going to be demolished. To some, this was the end of the world. Ken Bates purchased the piece of Wembley turf where the ball which Geoff Hurst struck had crossed the line. Colin Daniel, a Chelsea boy, once owned a pub near Wembley which hundreds of Chelsea fans had spilled out of that day, to confront the 'Boro boys who thought they were ambushing just another bunch of scarfers. Like the terraces, Wembley became a romantic memory, which never matched the reality of the pain and degradation we experienced there.

Nowadays, real life has come to the fore and many of the old faces are doing very well for themselves. The mentality needed to control people in a football crowd, and the element of taking risks, are good qualities for running a business. Also, these old fans have an unmistakable aura of being able to achieve against the odds.

Mickey Francis now runs a string of businesses in and around Moss Side, despite the club scene around Manchester being nicknamed Gunchester. Danny Harrison of West Ham is doing well in Tenerife, running clubs. Also making a success of himself in Tenerife is Paddy Maguire from Tottenham, who runs a restaurant business. Probably the most successful is the ex-ICF

Andy Swallow, who owns a record label. Ian Bean, who went around with the firm, started his own detective agency. He has since appeared on numerous TV shows.

All over, the rumour mill throws up stories of someone else making it big. Banana Bob, the famous Manchester cockney Red, wants to sell up his building company and emigrate to Spain, but he is still unsure of how the land lies after the well-reported Manchester United riot in Barcelona.

Hundreds of faces from different firms became big on the rave scene, and later on the club scene. Because of the huge geographical spread and the amount of foreign travel involved in football, many of the lads bump into each other at departure lounges in the most unlikely of locations, and while away a boring hour or two reminiscing about their exploits as adversaries.

One day, in the 1980s, the Ministry declared that hooligans all travelled first class and stayed at five-star hotels. With the elevation of their lifestyle, this came true. One summer in 1997, at a quiet bar in southern Spain, Eddie George, governor of the Bank of England, met a top Chelsea boy, a guvnor in his own right, but now able to converse about the relative merits of the European exchange rate mechanism. Eddie was unaware that the only European exchange his drinking partner had once been interested in was the exchange of blows with his foreign hooligan counterparts.

Terry Farley, who hung around with Maysie, became a DJ in and around the rave scene of the mid-'80s, eventually becoming one of the top names in that field. The boys became somebodies in the media's eyes. Gary Bushell used to hang around with the Charlton B mob, while Danny Baker made it big as a reporter and journalist, never losing his Millwall accent or attitude. Berating a stupid jobsworth who told him he couldn't film a news report on a stretch of pavement with the words, 'Don't you ever talk to me like that again. Do you understand?', he could have been outside the Cold Blow at Lane End with Puncho and the other Millwall boys, waiting for a tear-up.

Football is now big business, but lads will always be lads.

The boys still love their teams and follow their fortunes. The biggest hooligan story of the last few years featured the England team and I was fortunate to be there to see the action. Having invested my money in a business in the Far East, I am handily placed to watch when teams tour out there. Just before the European Championships, Terry Venables organised a tour of Hong Kong. More than anything else it seemed like a bonding exercise – all the rage in business nowadays. Sam Hickmott, Hickey's brother, Darryl Mann from Shrewsbury and myself travelled out to Hong Kong.

We knew Joe, the chief bartender at La Bamba's, and he recommended that we try the famous China Jump Bar, a classy clip-joint. Joe knew the head bartender there and he was passing us drinks, which the girls were sticking on the tabs of rich businessman, fleecing their expense accounts.

In the hurly-burly of the bar we were greeted by the cheeky Dennis Wise grin. Being Chelsea fanatics, it was good to see him. Dennis couldn't believe that we had come all this way to watch England, and was especially impressed that we were Chelsea fans.

'Fancy a beer, Dennis?' asked Sam.

'Leave it out, lads,' he said, pulling out a wad of notes, 'If you lot can spend fortunes coming all this way to watch us, the least we can do is show you some hospitality. I forbid any of you to buy a beer.'

'Send him over another drink,' added Wisey, pointing to Brian Robson. 'Got to keep the minder sweet, eh?'

After we'd been talking to Dennis for 20 minutes the club started filling up so the bouncers moved the England party into the VIP area, which was separate from the main bar. As we were with Dennis, we went with them. It was Gazza's birthday and Steve Howey's party trick was to take a gulp of beer and squirt everyone with it through the gap in his teeth. Gazza was staggering around ripping everyone's shirt off their backs.

'Rip my shirt off and I'll ring your geordie neck,' Sam told him. Gazza nodded in acknowledgement then lurched away, but later he caught Sam unawares when he was staggering around with Robbie Fowler, who was introducing Sam to everybody as his brother. Sam was signing autographs for Filipino girls who thought he was an England footballer.

Sheringham, later to get stick for being spotted in a nightclub, was standing at the bar, not drinking very much in comparison to the amounts the others were drinking. He was puzzled because we kept mocking him with the chant 'Yiddo, Yiddo'.

'Come on, lads, I'm not a Yiddo.'

'Yes, you are, you play for Spurs.'

Paul Ince was sitting brooding, looking over at us every once in a while. He didn't seem to like the fact that we were in the group. For the White Hart or the Lord Palmerston, read China Jump bar, Hong Kong. This could have been any pre-match drink and the fact that these lads now earned £20k per week became irrelevant when drink broke down the barriers which seem to have been erected between fans and players.

Ince walked over to the bar with Sol Campbell and barged through in a fairly aggressive fashion, unlike Sol, who was all smiles and could see that Teddy was making all of us laugh with his risqué jokes. Wisey laughed at Ince's behaviour. He sat down at the bar next to us.

'Wherever you go it's always the same: it's always West Ham,' said Darryl, referring to the fact that Ince used to play for West Ham. The funny part was that we were veterans of hundreds of pub brawls and now we were trying to have a fun time in peace, while someone held up as a role model for younger kids was the one being difficult. Role reversal at its most extreme.

Steve McManaman could have been any one of the thousands of scouse scallys we saw hanging around Lime Street. He kept coming over, grinning and putting on a stupid face, then walking away. For a moment, the bar became the last page of *Animal Farm*. This wasn't the England football team: it was our coach party on a Saturday night pub stop in a provincial town.

That night was made famous by the media, who managed to get a picture of them squirting vodka down each other's throats in a dentist's chair.

———

The boys still wear the famous Headhunters T-shirt, depicting an American GI walking through the dense jungle holding a severed Vietcong head in each hand. They still perform from time to time when necessary, and every so often the chaps turn up in Pattaya for a reunion. A crowd of us were sitting in Mistie's Go Go bar when three US marines came in. Two of them joined us at our table, while the other one went up to the bar where Gary Stevens, a Grimsby fan hailing from Cleethorpes, was standing. He looked at the T-shirt.

'Where you from, buddy?'

'England.'

'What's with the T-shirt?'

'Chelsea FC. Chelsea Headhunters.'

The marine was expecting more. It never came.

'I didn't see too many of you Brits in Vietnam.'

Gary Stevens turned to look at him. 'We didn't need to be there. The Vietcong gave you lot a kicking without our help.'

'Didn't want to get your Brit asses kicked, more like.'

With that, Gary nutted him full in the face. The marine went down in a crumpled heap, spark out. His two friends saw it: 'Geez. Did you see that? He slapped him with his face. That's incredible,' they exclaimed and went back to their drinks. The unconscious US marine was picked up and thrown out for causing a disturbance.

━━━━━━━

The 1980s are a long time past, and everybody is reminded of that when they look at the old newspaper clippings. The skinny youths who were able to run at will and exist on a diet of little or no sleep no longer resemble the overweight parodies of ourselves we have all now become. Past glories are relived at matches played in Riga, Marseilles and Stockholm, where Chelsea won the cup and the fans were praised for their good behaviour. The Russian poet must get his pen out and create a new aphorism to describe us.

'Welcome to hell,' announced the Turkish banner when Manchester United played in Istanbul. When Chelsea played there in October 1999, the Chelsea lads' banner said the same thing: 'Welcome to hell. We're not bothered.' Having been told for years by the Ministry that they were generals of terror who earned enough to travel the world creating terror and havoc, the fans finally became parodies of themselves. *The Sun* issued its 'Portrait of a Soccer Yob'. They roped in a top psychologist who kindly explained that the average soccer yob is oversexed, socially frustrated and on the lookout for violence. He has a low intelligence; he wants to feel important, but has grown up in a society which values the brainy more than the physically strong. Oh, yes . . . parents are sloppily permissive.

When England play anywhere in the world, the lurid headlines of trouble precede them. In Euro 2000 the authorities expected the worst. A simulated riot and fire drill intended as a test of security procedures was cut short when real hooligans turned up, and the 800 volunteers were augmented by a number of Feyenoord hard-core thugs. The Rotterdam police ended the exercise early.

In April 2000, the worst nightmare of all fans came true. Perhaps it was revenge against all those who had stepped too close to the edge and lived to tell the tale. In Istanbul, two Leeds fans were attacked and murdered the evening before the match against Galatasaray after an exchange of unpleasantries escalated into something far worse. Trivialising their deaths, UEFA declared that the match should be played anyway. When Italians died at Heysel it was seen as a tragedy caused by disgusting English hooligans and they banned all English clubs indefinitely, but when two innocent Leeds fans were butchered to death with knives and machetes they become only a statistic.

Only a fraction of anything that has ever been written by the Ministry about what really went on bears any resemblance to the truth, yet still they continue to rehash the same old clichés at regular intervals. In late 1998, the BBC commissioned a reporter to do an undercover exposé on the feared Chelsea Headhunters. In the opening sequence, Stuart Glass and Vincent Drake were cited as two of their notorious brethren. Who cared if it were true? The programme's factual content came under scrutiny immediately after, yet nobody stated that later on prime-time BBC TV to the nine million viewers.

In Euro 2000 in Belgium more words about hooliganism preceded the travelling lads than anyone had ever seen before. Most of the travelling fans were going on a weekend booze-up as England once more were drawn with their old adversary – Germany. So the authorities scheduled the match for a Saturday evening and they were surprised when the Saturday night specials descended on Brussels and, after a seven-hour drinking session, clashed with their German counterparts travelling across the border along with Belgian's finest riot police. No criminal trials this time, just hour after hour of video footage and banning orders, preventing known troublemakers travelling to the matches. This was put in place for the 2002 World Cup in Japan and South Korea with 1,007 English hooligans being served with banning orders. Cardiff City fans topped the banning chart – even though Cardiff fans are Welsh and I have never met any Welsh fans following England. Chelsea had 22 named hooligans and every one named on the BBC undercover programme received notification. Even though the tournament was bound to be free of Saturday Night specials – to travel to Japan meant you had to be in the Supertax bracket – the media hyped up the famous football hooligan. The lads who visit my bar every year stated that they were going on holiday to Thailand and were not intending to travel to a football match so their banning orders could not be served. On Saturday, 18 May 2002, *The Guardian* made myself and Hickey infamous for a day once again.

> Police have identified two convicted Chelsea football hooligans as being behind a lucrative fake football shirts scam that is set to hit the World Cup. Talks have already taken place between British police officials and their Japanese counterparts and kit manufacturers in an attempt to prevent hundreds of thousands of fake replica shirts flooding the tournament.
>
> According to reports they have spent the past few months getting fake replica shirts manufactured in Thailand. The two hooligans, who cannot be named for legal reasons, were part of the infamous Chelsea Headhunters gang but have since set up a bar in Thailand from which they are orchestrating the scam.
>
> The two were also spotted in Munich during England's World Cup qualifying match against Germany last September where they sold designer replica shirts ahead of the match. All the fake clothing had been manufactured in Thailand.

Police claim the pair will use their contacts in the hooligan community to sell the shirts and Japanese police and immigration officials have been warned to look out for dozens of known or suspected hooligans who will be attempting to enter the country via Thailand.

Behind the rhetoric was the hint that there were unofficial hit lists of people that had no convictions or spent convictions, yet were on lists of being suspected hooligans. And so it came to pass, as in the weeks leading up to the World Cup England fans not officially banned were denied entry to Japan. Two fans from Derby were sent back to Istanbul while others were just sent back to England. No doubt that they were not served banning orders because they would have seen their evidence tested in court and another plank of their anti-hooligan plans might have been thrown out by the judiciary. The funny part was that the old faces were indeed just that and age had expanded their midriffs alarmingly. The British Embassy in Tokyo were sufficiently alarmed by all the television reporting about the impending arrival of the English fans that they issued a leaflet to local shopkeepers to avoid misunderstandings. Under the heading 'You might feel frightened by their big bodies...' it contained such words of wisdom as:

> Trying to Communicate; memorising just a few phrases of English such as 'Welcome', 'Can I help you?' and 'England are a great team' can make quite a difference. What is an England Supporter? The behaviour of England supporters is different from that of football fans in Japan. Before the start of the game they gather in bars, parks and open spaces where they display their flags. While drinking beer and singing they raise their expectations for the match. By wearing their England shirts they express their pride in their mother country.

They then went on to explain how England fans discuss the match afterwards over another beer. 'Some supporters are very noisy and you might feel threatened by their large numbers.' Quite right too. The sight of thousands of Japanese sitting in the stands for the match against Sweden dressed in England shirts with 'Beckham' on the back terrified the average Englishman. Okay, so they didn't quite have the hang of singing 'No Surrender to the IRA', but in every other aspect they believed that they were following England.

Because of my contacts in Hong Kong and Thailand I was in a good position to help people out with travel information and obtaining match tickets, plus travel to Tokyo from UK via Thailand is cheaper than flying direct to Japan from England. It soon reached the UK newspapers and British police, who put a whole new slant on it.

> SOCCER THUGS PLAN TO SNEAK INTO JAPAN
> English police are to mount a security operation in Thailand following fears that known or suspected hooligans will try to travel from there to Japan for the World Cup. NCIS have been monitoring the activities of two men who now run a bar in Thailand and are reported to be organising trips to Japan. The two were leaders of Chelsea's Headhunters gang which orchestrated football violence during the 1980s but have been based in Thailand during the past five years.
>
> Bryan Drew, head of NCIS warned that potential troublemakers planning to go to Japan would be subject to rigorous security checks.

On a sunny Thursday morning a posse of stern-looking Thai police in dark glasses screeched up outside the bar and jumped out to be met by the quizzical looks of three English guys having a quiet beer in the heat. Ten seconds later a van load of army pulled up and spilled out. They were looking for the army of English hooligans and hundreds of thousands of fake shirts. Apart from the replica England shirts being worn by the bar staff they left rather bemused. Making replicas is part of the Thai economy so I have no doubt they were completely untroubled by the whole affair, while some junior clerk in the English embassy in Bangkok had been inundated with fax messages for the past week and had to be seen to act. Tokyo TV, based in London, spent a frantic few weeks before the World Cup going round interviewing as many of the writers of books on football fans as they could. One of the writers passed them a card of the Dog's Bollocks bar and told them to give me a call to arrange an appointment for an interview.

Unfortunately, they turned up uninvited early one evening and started photographing people. They then stuffed a microphone and camera in the faces of some of the banned lads, asking them ignorant intrusive questions. They were asked to leave, then they set up on the pavement opposite and continued filming. Considering this harassment the lads took matters into their own hands and the crew were given a beer shower and a friendly slap. Further up the road one of lads squirted pepper spray at them. Hickey, as is his wont, was fined 1,000 baht the next day for throwing beer. 'Just like the early '70s: abuse the media and fined a tenner,' was how he put it.

As I was not on any official banning list I decided to try and gain entry to Japan to watch the Argentina match along with eleven other lads. After a six-and-a-half-hour flight from Bangkok on Air Nippon, I was making my way towards immigration when two English police officers from the West Midlands Police appeared from behind a pillar and pulled Geordie Sam and myself to one side. After looking at our passports they sent us on our way with a cheery, 'No problem lads.' As I approached the white entry in Japan line and the unsmiling Mr Inscrutable at immigration two men appeared and ushered us into a room. After looking at our passports for an eternity they started asking us lots of dumb questions. 'How much do you drink?' 'How often do you drink?' 'Do you go out drinking together?'

Our connecting flight was due in an hour and a half and they knew that. After an hour it was obvious that we were not going to be let out so I started taking the piss back.

'Aren't you going to ask me if I like karaoke?' I asked. This seemed to antagonise them.

Eventually, after four hours of torture I stated to them that I wasn't going to answer any more questions and they asked me their big question which they should have asked me four hours previously and then refused me entry.

'Why are you really here?'

'To see how many of you lot the Americans missed at Hiroshima and to collect my grandfather's toenails which one of you sadistic bastards pulled out.'

That was it. After being charged £150 for a security guard escort to go and purchase a McDonalds in the airport we filled in some paperwork and the most dangerous football hooligan in the world was escorted back to the plane by two Air Nippon security guards who were ex French Foreign Legionnaires. I was refused entry into Japan because I was undesirable. My date with destiny watching England play Argentina was to escape me. At least we were spared the wait at the departure gate because they took me straight out to the aeroplane where Sam and I got some funny looks from the waiting passengers. Our Legionnaire escorts never spoke more than two words the whole return trip. Back in Thailand they tried to get us deported once again back to the UK, but the Thai authorities were having none of it, so along with 500 other England fans we watched the match in the street outside my bar in Pattaya – The Dog's Bollocks. Three days after the match the local Thai English newspaper stated that the behaviour of those watching the match was boisterous but good-humoured.

The first reported trouble of the World Cup came two days before the Argentina match in a Tokyo curry house when some drunks staggered in and caused great offence with their constant bad language. An argument followed and the police almost got involved. The band were journalists following the English team.

Argentina meanwhile put their severe economic troubles to one side to prepare for the match against England. One fan summed it up: 'A victory against England is our only chance of becoming someone in the world. We are totally defeated as a nation at the moment.'

The Japanese must have realised the significance of this because the same day they announced that they had scrapped plans to rent a ferry to ship hooligans out of Sapporo, venue of the match between England and Argentina. 'Since no one was arrested at the past two matches we have decided to cancel our plan,' an official explained.

Meanwhile, in Moscow, crowds gathered around a giant screen reacted violently after their defeat to the Japanese and rioting broke out, with cars being burned, police officers seriously injured and one man kicked to death while the Argentina v. England match went off peacefully. It was the theme for the whole World Cup. At the end the police patted themselves on the back and stated what a great success their security measures had been. They could get away with it in Japan, but Europe, with its myriad of borders and free travel, would always be a different matter.

They still try and take the charisma out of what we did, to make us into lemmings for the camera lens – that is like trying to take the glamour out of war, but nobody can ever take the excitement out of what we had. Football, travel, confrontation, the comrades: it was the greatest roller-coaster ride ever. It was a culture which had no precedent, and subsequently was uncontrollable for a short while. It dwarfed everything which had preceded it. Then it all juddered to a halt of its own accord and most of us got off.

This is football hooliganism. To use the parlance of Hollywood in *The Man Who Shot Liberty Vallance*: 'When the truth becomes legend, print the legend'.